George Weaver

Looking forward for Young Men

Their Interest and Success

George Weaver

Looking forward for Young Men
Their Interest and Success

ISBN/EAN: 9783337372453

Printed in Europe, USA, Canada, Australia, Japan

Cover: Foto ©Suzi / pixelio.de

More available books at **www.hansebooks.com**

LOOKING FORWARD

FOR YOUNG MEN

THEIR INTEREST AND SUCCESS

BY

REV. GEORGE SUMNER WEAVER, D.D.

NEW YORK
FOWLER & WELLS CO.
775 BROADWAY
1891

PREFACE.

In the autumn of 1849, forty years ago, the author of this little volume wrote, at the suggestion of some young men he was teaching, a series of lectures which was published by Fowler & Wells in 1850, entitled Mental Science. In the summer previous, he wrote and gave as Sunday afternoon discourses to the young people of his congregation, a series of discourses which was published two years later by the same firm, under the title of Hopes and Helps for the Young. Now, in 1889, he writes for the young again, to be read by the children and grandchildren of those who read his first books, and to be published by the same firm. A profitable psychological study may be had by comparing this volume with those written forty years earlier.

The young we have always with us, and work for them will always be in order. The world's improvement must be made largely through them. They are the readiest to be instructed, the most susceptible to ennobling influences, and least hindered by prepossessions and prejudices. The hopes of the ages are in them, and those who are in sympathy with them can help humanity through them. The author acknowledges with pleasure that of all he has done in a many-sided life, that which he has done for the young has given him the best satisfaction. They have helped him while he has endeavored to help them. They have renewed his youth and given him inspiration, and now he joins with them to give a grand exit to the greatest century the world has seen. They are to be leaders in the great uplifts of the society that are to be. All hail to them and the centuries for which they are preparing. In the hope of joining with them to keep step to the music of human improvement and joy, the author asks once again to be admitted to their company and confidence.

G. S. W.

EAST PROVIDENCE, R. I., October, 1890.

CONTENTS.

LOOKING FORWARD

FOR YOUNG MEN.

CHAPTER I.

THE YOUNG MAN AND HIS PATRIMONY.

THE young man and his patrimony open for the first chapter of this volume two themes of large interest. There is no individual needier, or worthier of the best wisdom that can be given him, than the young man, because he is always an important element of society, the prospect and promise of the future, and a large factor in the hope of the world. A benefit to him is equally a benefit to the young woman who is to share with him his patrimony. Much is being done for her in these days, in the many ways in which her interests are cared for; and perhaps in no way can she be more effectually served than in what may be done to ennoble her coming companion. The greatest benefit to a woman is a worthy and suit-

able husband; so the greatest benefit to woman-
kind is to enrich the world with genuine men.

The young man, what is he? A new ship
freighting for a voyage of the world — a new
machine fitting for its place in the world's great
factory—a new institution organizing to compete
for enterprise and success in the world's affairs,
a new human being equipping for the battle of
life to win victory, or defeat according to his conduct of the battle. Human life is a battle, and
every man is a soldier enlisted for the war. He
cannot flee the ranks, nor employ a substitute,
nor turn back from the contest except at the
peril of defeat and disgrace. He is to make of
life a well-fought battle, or a shameful rout. The
choice is before him, and he is to take it deliber-
ately, with his eyes open, in his right mind, ac-
cepting the responsibility and consequences.

If life is a battle and every man a soldier, he is
drafted, not volunteered. He did not plan the
campaign of human life, nor arrange the necessity
of soldiership, nor have any voice in the question
whether he would have a part in it or not. Life
is not of our making. The first we know of it we
have it. It is forced upon us. We live before
we know it. Living is Providential—the gift of
others and not our choice. Something, therefore,
is back of us. Something gave us being and
drafted us into the inevitable campaign of life,

and that same something holds us to soldierly
duty and to loyal living at the peril of defeat.
Something of life is in our hands, but much of it
is shaped for us, and the whole of it is under a
Superintendency that watches its processes and
estimates its results, quite differently often from
what we do. It is important that we recognize at
the outset the fact that "there is back of us and
over us and in us," Something not of ourselves
that we must obey, Something that makes intelligent demands upon us and holds us to ac-
countability and duty. We do not make our
duties, at any rate, only a part of them. For the
most part, we are put into our places and our
duties are forced upon us, even as is life itself.
The necessities, discipline, and laws of life we did
not make, but the tactics, conduct, and drill of
life are largely in our own hands; yet there is so
much of it preordered, or directed by an invisible
Hand, that we can scarcely call it our own. It
seems largely to be given to be lived for the Giver.
With life, are given the laws of its being, the
powers of mind and body that come with it, the
stirring incentives of love and honor and duty
that move us to action, the world and its rich
opportunities for growth and enjoyment, country,
home. and friends and all that come with them to
invite to the feasts of honor and pleasure. All
these and more than can be catalogued are the

gifts of a paternal Hand to every young man.
Indeed, we are born to a splendid *patrimony*, an
estate of uncounted wealth.   Body, mind, world,
country, society, relationships, institutions, the
universe about us, the laws within us, God over
us, the immortality that we trust is before us,
constitute the estate we have inherited.   Is not
all this worth living for, to use and honor with a
splendid service?   Does not such a patrimony indicate the wealth, dignity and goodness of the
paternal Giver? and also the capacity and worth
of the untried mind and heart that has been
favored with such a rich estate?   No youth has
any right to count himself poor who is born to
such a patrimony.   No youth should feel orphan-
ized whose Father has enriched him with such
wealth.   No one should feel lonely, or discouraged
in the midst of such company and such abundance.   At the very start life opens to the grandest opportunities.   Surely its meaning must be
sublime and its progress and outcome ought to be
honorable.

This estate is twofold.   Part of it is *in* the
young man himself; part of it is outside of
him; and the value of each is enhanced by the
other.

And what is the part of the estate within himself?   This too consists of two parts, his body and
mind.   And they enhance each other's value.

Body and mind make up the man of this world,
body and mind in a terrestrial partnership. Body
and mind are enlisted together for the campaign
of time. Body and mind do life's work in mutual
dependence and helpfulness. Body and mind in
their subtle and marvellous union constitute the
personal estate which each young man receives
from the Hand that wrought so wondrously the
powers of his being. And what a being! Who
can estimate properly the capacity for action, and
honor, of the young man, and the grand significance of the career that is before him? What
beauty and power of body! What elasticity of
muscle! What strength and toughness of sinew!
What hardness of bone, suppleness of action, and
tenacity of life! What keenness of sense, what
strength, what ability to endure! What robust-
ness of health, what vigor of constitution! What
richness of blood! What vital forces animate it
through and through! What nerves of sensibility
thread all its parts! No less a thing of power
than of beauty; no less a thing of wonder than of
art; no less a marvel than a model of mechanism!
The body of youth, it is indeed "fearfully and
wonderfully made."

And this marvellous form of magnetic matter
—this animated Apollo, this instrument of a
thousand strings and more uses is a *gift* to every
young man from its Maker—a gift conferred with-

out the asking—a gift which in its very excellence
puts it at the head of created things.

And yet wonderful and valuable as is this body,
it is but the least part of that inestimable personal patrimony which the young man receives at
his enlistment into life's campaign; for into this
body is put a power of mind—a capacity for intelligence, affection, and honor that allies him
with the Divine, that gives him the command of
all earthly things—the dominion of the animated
world. This body is charged with mind to reason, command, and execute, to use all material
things for its benefit and develop society, character, manhood. It is mind that makes the man.
Beautiful, nimble, powerful as is the body, it is
a toy or tyrant without the mind to control
it to noble ends. It is the mind that gives the
body value and dignity. It is the mind that enriches life, that gives the charm of home and
honor to noble public service. The mind is the
man — the thinker, inventor, mechanic, artist,
scholar, statesman, preacher. It is the mind that
holds the wealth and power of life. Body and
mind joined in a this-world partnership to promote the great ends of life, are the personal patrimony which every youth receives with which to
begin life. And is this all? No; for a sphere of
action, a world in which to live and the hope of an
immortal one to come with it to give opportunity

as grand as may be desired. This is the young man's outfit for life.

But this is not all; for man has the capacity to coöperate with his kind for mutual enjoyment and benefit, and thus produce home, society, country, and all the fine enrichment of life that comes from them. By joining hand with hand and mind with mind in great numbers, the marvels of society grow up around him, to offer him their multiform advantages. This power of co-operation is one of the efficient sources of human greatness and enjoyment. If each man had to live and work alone, had to use his mind and body all for himself and by himself, could call in no help from his kind, could add no power to his own, could not multiply himself by union with others like him, how insignificant he would be in comparison with what he now is. He would be a Samson shorn of his locks. The linking power that makes long chains of humanity, the weaving power that makes great webs of our kind, the multiplying power that combines vast numbers of men, are what make society and all its marvel-lous possibilities of intelligence, usefulness and greatness. The parent coöperates with the child to grow a man or woman. The teacher coöperates with the pupil to make the scholar. The builder coöperates with the man needing a house in its production. The tailor coöperates with the man

needing garments to clothe him. The merchant co-
operates with his customers to get his goods into
use. The banker coöperates with those needing
his help. The author coöperates with his publisher and readers to mingle his thoughts with
theirs. The preacher coöperates with those hun-
gry for the bread of spiritual life. So it is all the
way around in this great combination which we
call society. Coöperation is its law, which is to
be carried out more and more perfectly till it
shall come to be full of mutuality and helpfulness. Men have coöperated in war, and will for
some time to come. But its terrible destructive-
ness and folly will by and bye teach them better,
when they have combined to learn the lessons of
peace. Then they will coöperate in arbitration to
settle their difficulties. Men have combined in
many forms of iniquity and do still, but the moral
light of the better combinations of men, and the
evils of iniquity becoming more and more apparent are teaching them that the true coöperation
is in things virtuous and useful. This great law
is working the marvels of social advancement in
the great world into which the young man is born
to his patrimony.

The spring of this wide coöperation is *friendship*, not selfishness as some have said. Friendship is a part of the human mind and a strong
part. Human nature is intensely social. To be

deprived of fellow-intercourse is held as a great evil. We would hardly call one a man in whose heart there beats no throb of friendship. We would not want for a neighbor the man who responds not to the kinship of humanity. We would prefer not to have even the acquaintance of the man who is nobody's friend. This linking quality, this binding sentiment which makes all the world akin, is as strongly dominant in young men as in any class of humanity. Though it sometimes operates for evil when it links them with evil associates, it is one of the hooks to which the wires of good influences are to be hitched, one of the storage batteries which holds the magnetism of the best things. This ground principle of friendship out of which grow the infinite affiliations and coöperations of humanity is a part of the young man's patrimony. It links him to humanity, and is the subtle element which makes possible to him a clear knowledge of his fellowmen. It is charged with the insight of human nature and is full of the amenities which make agreeable our human intercourse. This is a gift of the Infinite Love.

Now, there are some practical things to be deduced from these considerations, which are helpful to the young man in enabling him to adjust himself properly to the life-work upon which he has entered. In the first place, he is in friendly

relations with his fellow-men. There is *honor* in
friendship, and that honor will not permit a slight
or forgetfulness of friends.

There is *justice* too in friendship which recog-
nizes the worth and benefit of friends and does
not fail to render meet acknowledgments for
favors. It makes full returns.

Then there is *gratitude* in friendship, that *feels*
obligations, and expresses in words and acts its
reciprocal esteem.

Now, keeping these good principles in mind
which every young man means to live by in his
faithfulness to his friends, how ought every one
to feel toward his first, great, Supreme Friend
from whom he has received his great patrimony?
What is due, according to these just principles, to
the Infinite Love for these inestimable favors?

As a matter of *honor*, how should a young man
begin and conduct his life in relation to the
Friend of all friends? Will neglect of his just
requirements, profanity of his name, denial of his
authority, repudiation of his law, resistance of his
spirit, opposition to his righteous rule, cancel the
debt of honor to him with which every young
man starts in life? Every young man would de-
spise himself if he should bandy his mother's
name in joke or ribaldry, or if he should forget
to remember with esteem and tenderness her toils
and good offices in his behalf. We all feel that

there should be both honor and principle in friendship, and that they apply as well to the Unseen
Friend as to any in the flesh. He who is unjust
with God cherishes the principle which may make
him unjust with men. Ingratitude to the Great
Giver of good is likely to be the root of ingratitude to every giver of good. Falsity in our relation to the Divine goodness may be the seed of
falsity in relation to all good actions. Infidelity
to God may be the germ of infidelity to man.
Just here is a principle of the utmost importance
to young men. Too many young men think they
can jest about God, and coquette with infidel notions and not be harmed in moral character or
life. This is a sad mistake; for just in this is the
beginning of irreverence and moral debasement.

The friendship of young men is beautiful, and
it enters largely into their character and lives.
And nothing is more important than that it shall
be pure. And to have it pure and influential,
nothing contributes more than genuine gratitude
to God for the many and grand gifts of his wisdom and love. There is nothing manly in irrelig-
iousness, but always something promotive of character in sincere reverence and gratitude.

The conclusion, therefore, is forced upon us that
a debt of reverent and grateful obligation rests
upon the young man who receives his patrimony
of body, mind and world of men and things, from

2

the Infinite Giver of all good, and that a rightful recognition of this obligation is the fountain of both genuine morality and religion.

It is evident that the chief part of his patrimony is himself. How he should hold it, what do with it, what advantages ought to accrue to him from it, and what service it should be to others, are points which will be somewhat considered in the succeeding chapters.

CHAPTER II.

THE YOUNG MAN AND HIS FRIENDS.

In introducing this subject, immensely important to young life, it may be well to consider,
first, what view of life shall be taken, whether
hopeful or dismal, whether manly or brutal,
whether it shall have an upward or a downward
look, an upward or a downward grade. The tendency—the grade of life will show itself as clearly
in its *friends* as in any other way. "Birds of a
feather flock together." A man is as well known
by the company he keeps as by the words he
speaks, or acts he does.

The start in life is important; it gives direction,
set, tendency, the shaping influence. To start
with base views of life is to set the impulses, ambitions, desires, to low aims, and put the social
nature at the same grade. To start with high
views of life, is to give aspiration to all the energies and to stimulate a craving for friends and
associates who are moved with similar uplooking
impulses. As the rifle points, so goes the ball.
As the first step directs, so follow the succeeding
steps. The start is immensely important. To

start right is to get the impulse and push of all one's energies to bear him on and up, and to bring to his aid friends who will join their forces to his. To start wrong is to put one's whole nature behind him to bear him down and to draw other similar natures to aid in the downward movement. To start with idlers, vagrants, drinkers, gamblers, and learn first their low notions of life and what it is for and how to be conducted, he gets their bent and impulses in himself and the heavy weight of their coarseness and brutality added to bear him down their way. He not only gets inoculated with their evil, but he gets them for friends who prove a still heavier weight of evil. If he starts with the pure and fair-minded who see life a good opening for all good aims and enterprises, and makes them his friends, his course at once takes direction from his start and is borne on by all there is in him and them to press him forward. He adds his friends to himself to give him success. Surely the start in life is vital and tells mightily upon the whole succeeding career. If the start is wrong, the first lessons will be wrong and they must be unlearned, or the whole following life will be wrong. To unlearn is harder than to learn; to turn back is harder than to go forward. To start wrong is worse than not to start at all. "Be sure you are right, then go ahead." Therefore, the first thing is *to start right.*

But we do not get our first start *alone*. We are linked with others. Some friend aids us, gives the direction, furnishes the force that starts us on. This first friend is one of the most important we ever have. The first friend is a great help, or hurt. If the first friend puts poison into the cup of our life, who will take it out? If the first friend gives a wrong direction to our easily directed steps, who will turn them back to the right? If the first friend gives us false views of what we are in the world for, who will correct them? The hand of the first friend is on the rudder of a new ship. The influence of the first friend is a mightily telling one. The young man does not choose his first friend. That friend is oftenest a mother. But mothers too often are not wise, too often are weak and unequal to the great task of giving wise direction to the lives that come into their hands. But, be it a mother, or some one else, that friend puts more into the new life than any other. In a silent, yet effectual way that friend becomes the feather's weight that turns the scale.

At this early hour in the young life, how happy if a cheerful spirit, a sunny temper, a high-toned view of life and its great aims and work, shall impress themselves upon the facile young mind and quicken it with their love of bright and generous things. There is far more in first impressions

than many people think.   They are seeds of great
things to come. "Just as the twig is bent the
tree's inclined" is a truth so important that it has
become almost scripture in the philosophic mind.

This world into which the young mind opens is
one of beauty and grandeur—a world of sunshine
and flowers, of buds and fruits, of little seeds and
great growths, of oceans from little fountains, of
empires from trifling beginnings, of giants from
helpless babes; it is a world of work and rest, of
duty and pleasure, of society and solitude, of
change and stability, of varitey and sameness,
of common and rare things, of many employments
and rich opportunities, all affording rich instruction to the teachable mind, profitable enjoyment
to the virtuous heart, and grand success to the
soul keyed to the many-toned music of its harmonious whole. How happy if the young man's
first friend shall put him into early harmony with
the spirit and meaning of this grand and many-
sided world, all of whose sides reflect like a diamond the light of the great universe about it.

So the first friend cannot do better than to in-
spire in the young mind hopeful and courageous
views of the life before it. Life is not to be
dreaded but welcomed. A good life is often half
made by getting a happy view of its good uses to
begin with. Fortunate is a young man whose
first friends so shape his life that it shall get a

good start without being poisoned with evil, or turned into downward ways. These friends are parents, brothers and sisters, schoolmates and associates and such as are truly helpful in their influence.

How many a parent, teacher, minister, friend, has given the timely word or influence which has early won the young heart to the best things and made it the planting ground of all good principles! These first friends are often mighty friends in the power of good influence, to whom is due more in the making of great and good men, than to any later friends. Great men are oftener made great by what influences them before than after twenty-one. Most true men get the set toward true manliness in boyhood and get it by the true friends of that early period. It is hard to straighten the bent twig, hard to turn from his misdirected course the impetuous youth. Those who early train the young mind have the best chance of putting it into wisdom's ways. Unspeakably important are the earliest friends of men. They are not of their own choosing, but they prove their friendliness by the good they do. Their work in the young man, he must accept or reject, when his mind matures enough for personal judgment upon it. The time comes and comes pretty early, when he begins to be his own man, begins to decide on the right and wrong of conduct, begins to form opinions, estimate characters and determine who shall be his friends. This is a critical time and often shapes all that follows it. If now his first friends shall have so helped him, or his own inclinations so direct him that he chooses wisely so that he gets help and not hindrance from them, he has made a good beginning. Just here he may well consider before he acts. The choice of friends is hardly second in importance to any other choice he has to make. Every young man must have friends, but who and what they shall be are as important as any questions he has to settle. The old saying that a man is known by the company he keeps, indicates how his reputation is to be affected by his friends. It is equally true that a man is made in part by his friends. He accepts something of their opinions, conforms somewhat to their principles, is won somewhat to their habits and takes on something of their characters. To have a friend is to go part way to him and subject ourselves to his influence. We do not have friends to resist them, but to welcome them to confidence and consideration, and therefore to influence in our lives. If our friend is cheerful, he makes us more so than we should be without him; if he is honest he braces up our integrity; if he is well bred, he helps our manners; if he is good-tempered, he benefits our disposition; but if he is the opposite of all these

in these particulars he is harmful to us. If he is
profane he will not improve our speech, nor our
taste for good language; if he is skeptical he will
not help our faith; if he is coarse he will not
polish our manners; if he is selfish and mean he
will weaken our moral force. We ought to have
friends for the good they will do us, not for any
evil we may get from them. We are foolish if
we accept as friends those who have the small-
pox or any contagious disease. Evil is contagious,
and to choose for friends those who are subject to
it, is to choose it. We do not, therefore, want to
cast our pearls before the swine of our friends;
indeed we do not want for friends those who keep
swine. We do not want to lean on such faulty
supports. If we ride in a defective carriage, we
may expect a break-down. If we drive a balky
horse we may stop just when we want to go on.
Defective friends are frail carriages, are balky
horses. We do not have friends for dangers, or
burdens, but for benefits. No young man can
afford to have friends who would bring him bad
associates, show him the way to bad places, or
familiarize him with bad principles. He cannot
afford to have friends with bad manners, much
less with bad characters, or speech, or habits.
Such friends are a load he would better not try
to carry. He may give to paupers, and tell the
wicked to repent, but he would better not make

up the list of his friends from these classes. If
he does not accept the bad in the characters or
habits of his friends, they will familiarize him
with it, make him tolerant of it, and bring him
down to a level with it.

To say the least his chosen friends should be
as good as himself, of as good blood, intelligence,
character, habits and aim in life. There is neither
wisdom nor good taste in going down to get
friends. Friendship is winning and if its objects
are below us, it is likely to take us down to them.

And friendship is often *costly*, especially when
it is not wisely formed. If for an unwise friendship, we take on as a penalty, a habit that shall
make us its slave for life, that shall pilfer money
from our pockets every day, that shall unnerve
our muscles, stupefy our brains, injure our health,
unsteady our purposes and unman our characters,
it is at a fearful cost. How do young men learn
the use of tobacco? That plant is offensive to
everything that lives, except the tobacco worm.
It nauseates and poisons every natural organism
that attempts to use it, either to smoke, chew, or
snuff. It can be borne only after a hard breaking
in—a persevering discipline—a kind of martyr-
dom. And when one is broken in so thoroughly
as to get the tobacco habit, he is ever after taxed
a number of cents a day to keep it up, making a
bill of several thousand dollars in a life-time—a

handsome little competency for a moderate family, is steadily reduced in health and strength and is made filthy and disagreeable to all people of natural senses and delicate tastes. No one breaks himself in to this habit of his own accord and all by himself. He submits to the hard ordeal through the influence of friends. It is a social habit, one of the penalties of perverted friendship, and costly in many ways. The wide prevalence of the tobacco habit is a heavy weight on our civilization, as well as an unspeakable disagreeableness

How does the young man learn to drink? Here is an evil of immense magnitude—largely a man's evil habit—not woman's, which is so destructive that manhood goes rapidly down before it, that character pales in its presence, that gentility and respectability yield to as paper to the flame, that talent and learning are not proof against, that political parties serve as slaves, and legislatures and congresses take off their hats and manhood to, that even not a few churches are silent before, and which throttles the daily press of all countries—an evil that is the laboring man's greatest enemy, the seed of immense vice and crime, the peril of the home, the heartache of woman, which carries down to annual death, or a worse destruction, a quarter of million of men. Cost! Who can tell its cost in money, character, grief and

men? And yet a new army of young men every
year learn to drink. They keep the army full
that is marching down the drunken decline. Sad
and awful procession, trampling under foot that
manhood made in the Divine image. Young men
learn to fill the deluded ranks at the wine cup and
beer mug, led there by the friends they have
chosen to be deluded by. This too is a social
evil. There is stimulation, delusion, mirth and
frenzy in it. The young learn the habit of their
older friends, then join together in the dementing
guzzle. A kind of immoral fatality, like that of
idolatry, slavery, bigamy in the olden times, has
made the drink dementation popular and given
it its financial, political and social foothold of
men. Its root is more in friendship than anywhere else, the perversion, the misuse, the degradation of friendship. Young friends do not *mean*
to go to evil when they drink together, but they
do none the less cherish the great iniquity and
prostitute friendship to the ruin of men. No boy
starts out from his home for the saloon the first
time alone. Some friend who has learned the
way of some other friend must lead him. It is
the supposed friendship in the saloon that makes
it enticing. Divide it into stalls and make every
man drink alone; forbid sociability; separate
friends the moment they enter the door and let
nothing but drink be the attraction and young

men would not go there. There is nothing enticing in drink at the beginning. The habit has to
be formed by effort and practice. At length the
stimulation leads on the appetite to contribute to
the craze and the whole man becomes other than
himself—an alcoholic victim, a pitiable wretch
who has joined the army that is destroying our
civilization. No greater mistake can any young
man make than to learn to tipple. The only safe
way is to taste not, touch not, handle not the intoxicating draught. Even in its mildest form it
is the beginning of evil. It deludes when it says
there is no harm in a little. The little is the beginning of the whole evil. The great waste, the
awful desolation of the drunken ruin, begins in
the little. Say no at once to any friendly suggestion to drink. There is perfect safety in perfect
abstinence.

Other evil courses are entered in much the
same way by the enticement of friends. No boy
takes up rowdyism and low life of his own accord.
The suggestion comes from his friendly relation
with other boys, and usually some older boy leads
the way. No boy sits down by himself and de-
liberately plans mischief which he proposes to
execute alone. It was never known that a college
boy got up and executed a college prank all by
himself. Pranks, mischiefs, scandals, evil habits
and ways come very largely from unwise friend-

ships, or friendships unwisely conducted. Misfortunes, loss of character, property, place and reputation, are often due to friends over-trusted. It is true that there are few good things more dangerous and costly than friendship. It is the open door to a multitude of misfortunes. Unwise friendship has ruined more young men than any other one thing. It is the gilded, slippery incline that glides gently down to unexpected woes. And it is not because friendship is bad; for in itself it is not bad, but good. Nearly all evil is perverted good. It is only when it is unwise that it leads to bad results.

Friendship in itself is the very sunshine of life. It gives us the daisies and buttercups that bloom by our common pathways and makes warm, fragrant and songful the otherwise acrid atmosphere of necessity and duty. We could not live without friends. We need not. Only be wise in the choice of friends and we are safe—aye, and more than safe; for while it is true that bad friends are burdens and stumbling-blocks, it is equally true that good ones are helps. They are not only comforts and joys, but solid supports to our plans and purposes, real forces added to our strength. Society is possible only on the basis of genuine friendship. Families, schools, churches, hold together chiefly by the cement of friendship. Business rests on it not a little; for how much it aids the merchant to sell his goods, the physician to get and hold his patients, the mechanic to make his work acceptable, the banker to hold the confidence of his customers, and every business man to get on well with those with whom he deals. The man without friends in a community has a poor business prospect there. It is true there is business and success in friends. They are the rounds in the ladder of success. The good trades, callings and professions are friendly helps to each other. Politicians help one another and make heavy drafts on personal friendships in their partisan plans. Community makes a division of labor that its work may be done cheaper and better, on the principle of friendly relationship. The different vocations coöperate for mutual benefit, because in trustful friendship they confide in one another. Our civilization has grown up on the basis of friendship—helping one another in mutual confidence. And on this basis it must rid itself of its great evils, must beat its swords into ploughshares and learn war no more. The nations are friendly and must learn to be more so, that they may make a freer exchange of benefits and be mutual aids in their great governmental and social offices.

So it is clear that the young man should have friends. The instinct of his nature to confide in those nearest to him and link his interests with them, is right. He should not be an iceberg chill-

ing everybody that comes near him; nor a recluse
shut up from a friendly world; nor a porcupine
sticking quills into everybody that comes near
enough to him. It should be one aim of his life
to make friends and hold them. It should even
be a part of his business. One has scarcely a right
to live in this world without being friendly and
making friends. But then, one need not be a
sponge and imbibe muddy water just as readily
as clear. One need not forget that people are different, and some of them will harm us with their
friendships. One need not go into evil places
hunting friends, nor follow friends into dark and
dangerous ways. One need not lay aside his judgment, nor his moral sense, nor his taste, nor his
respect for a good name, when he chooses his
friends, nor in his association with them. In
nothing does he want these good qualities more
than in his friendships. A man is known by his
friends and he is influenced by them, and made
like them. A man goes up or down according to
the help, or hindrance he gets from his companions.
All important is it, therefore, to have the right
kind of friends—wholesome friends, good-man-
nered friends, good-principled friends, good-speak-
ing friends. All important is it too, that we keep
level-headed, pure-hearted, fair-dealing in our
friendships.

The young man who starts in life with such first

friends, and such of his own choosing, has in one respect made the best kind of a start, and other needful things being equal to these, is almost sure of a successful, honorable and happy life.

3

CHAPTER III.

THE NEEDED FRIENDS AND HOW TO GET AND KEEP THEM.

IN the last chapter, the start in life, its relation to others, the world in which it is lived, the first friend, the chosen friends, their influence, costliness, helpfulness, as well as their need, were somewhat considered. But the general subject would be left in a too crude and external shape, unless another chapter were added which should go more to the root of the matter and consider the more inward things which relate to *character* and *manhood*.

The proposition will not be disputed that the young man must have friends—not any kind of friends, that like burrs may happen to stick to him, or like leeches may want to suck his blood, but *good* friends who have not only the quality of adhesiveness, but the strength and soul of helpfulness and honor. Now the question is, how to get them? This is vital. Every young man wants many things that he does not quite see how to get. He wants money and much of it, but how to get it is another thing. He wants honorable position, but about its attainment he is not so clear. He wants success, but the way to it is the problem he is anxious to have solved. So he wants friends, one of the best helps to attain these other much-coveted things and without which they cannot be attained, and *how to get them*, is the matter he is now invited to consider.

And to begin with, he should not be discouraged with the idea that they are hard to get. All the best things have been had by others, and are still to be had on their own terms. The kind of friends he most needs are not shy, or evasive, or unap-proachable. They are as solicitous to come to him as he is to have them. They will not keep away from him, nor hedge up his way to them. He is ever to them an object of abiding interest, and they wait for the opportunity to serve him. Suc-cess may be hard to attain; honorable position may be far off and high up; wealth may be wholly out of his reach; but good friends are at hand for every young man who will show himself worthy of them. If he is poor he can get them; if he is without learning he can get them; if he is of hum-ble parentage he can get them; though deformed, and personally unattractive he can get them. They are all about him and wait to be captured by him. They even crave the privilege of being his friends. The best men and women of the

world are looking to the young men about them
for a hint of what they can do for them, for a sign
of their readiness to be befriended. The hope of
the world is in the young man, and all the wise
and good know it. They are building institutions
for him, making homes, estates, all the good things
of our civilization for him, and are anxious beyond
expression that he shall be worthy of it all and fit
himself to use it well and pass it on unharmed
and improved to his posterity. What, then, shall
he do to make it clear to these waiting friends
that they can trust and honor him and pass over
to him gladly all their possessions?

1. The first thing he has to be, is a friend to
everybody; the first thing he has to do is to be
friendly himself. He must put the principle of
the golden rule in practice, and be to others what
he wants them to be to him. He must carry a
friendly face, tongue, hand and spirit, be a friend,
as the thing that is easy, natural, always foremost. As a boy he must be friendly to his mates,
teachers, neighbors, so that instead of being afraid
of him, they all meet him gladly, and count him
the joy, rather than the dread of the neighborhood.
The man begins in the boy. All who know a
worthy young man, like to remember that as a
boy he was equally worthy. It makes their friendship for him all the tenderer and more confiding.
The boy begins to make friends for his manhood,

and if he is the boy that the wise and good honor he makes a host of them.

2. Then back of this outward manner and conduct, he must show in his every-day life that he means well to everybody; that he is sincere and genuine; that he takes nothing not his own; that he does nothing vicious, or dishonorable; that he shuns bad company and places; that his tongue catches no bad words, nor his disposition bad tempers; that his feet run not in foolish ways, nor he find pleasure in foolish people. His daily life must be so manly and fair that good people will not only be not afraid of him, but like him and be drawn to him. Such genuineness will win friends who will themselves be genuine and real helps in pursuit of the best things.

3. He must not only be without bad habits and manners, but he must have positive virtues, be a positive man, stand for definite opinions and count for a specific intellectual and moral sum. He must have convictions of his own for the right on the great questions, have his reasons for them, and be pronounced for sobriety, virtue, patriotism and religion—an open, honest advocate of the clean and of good report.

If he talks down the good things which the best men of all ages have honored; if he discounts virtue; sees the prizes of life in pleasure; honors chiefly the sensuous and selfish in philosophy and

conduct; questions the facts of the higher life and
an unselfish virtue; and so gives the weight of his
convictions and influence to the materialistic view
of life, it will be certain that he will shut off from
his enjoyment and profit the best friends and
friendship of this world.   He thus chooses a lower
grade, casts his lot with those like himself, and
discards the higher range which he ought to keep
open to him.

It is great presumption in a young man of little
knowledge and experience to sit in judgment on
the wisdom of the ages, to oppose the cherished
and sacred things which saints have lived to glorify and martyrs have died to honor.   And that
presumption is as much in his own way as his
verdict against sacred things.   If, where the greatest and best men are reverent, he is flippant; if
where the wisest walk with bated breath, he is
self-conscious and has a sneer for aspiring faith
and humble prayer; if, where the profoundest
scholarship and philosophy are modestly inquiring, and the richest souls are craving guidance that
human help cannot give, he is self-assured and
pronounces all such humility and seeking for light,
cant and foolishness, he, by this very attitude of
mind, repels the friendly help he most needs and
invites the bravado and conceit of the coarse and
earth-minded.   Nothing is more distasteful to
truly noble minds, than that conceit of capacity

which judges of profound things without exami-
nation, and sacred and spiritual things without
soul-experience. Modesty in the young mind is
so delightful to the wise and good that they are
drawn to it as steel to a magnet. The inquiring
mind, and humble spirit and believing soul, are
so becoming to early years, that the youth who
possesses them is a joy to the best friends he could
possibly have, and by these he wins a friendship
worth more than gold to him. Good men admire
thoughtfulness and good thinking. They even
like to see the young have a good degree of independence in their thinking. They admire clear,
strong intelligence. They like the young mind
that can see through sham and pretence, that refuses the hoary wrong and accepts the new right,
that repudiates the ancient falsehood and embraces
the fresh truth. They like the young enthusiast
of progress, the young searcher for what is true
and useful, the young soul that is on fire for improvement, which wants to *run* with animation,
and not *plod* with dulness, in the way of advancing light and liberty and right living. Such young
minds win upon all good people with a strange
power, and such people befriend them with alac-
rity of joy. There is a vast difference between
the honest, morally earnest and reverent aspirant
for the best things, even though he discounts ancient creeds and customs, and the coarse and pur-

blind iconoclast who tears down all ancient altars
and builds no new ones in their stead.

The young of our time are peculiarly exposed
to this iconoclastic spirit which puts assumption
in the place of study, bravado and sensual conceit
in the place of reverent seeking, which puts out
the old lights and puts nothing that is light in
their places.

Oh that the bright, strong young men of to-day
could see that in the thoughtful, aspiring, reverent and believing mind, are the qualities that win
and hold the noblest friends! Doubt of the best
things is not attractive of the best souls. Whoever begins the life of manhood in infidelity to the
highest things, will be very likely to become infidel to the common things which are true and good,
and will be sure to miss the friendship of those
who can do him the most good. Blight in the top
of the tree shows disease in the heart and root.
There is a field for thoughtfulness right here which
must be left to those of discriminating mind.

4. The young man, to make the best friends,
must be manly—clear through and everywhere, he
must be a man. Even a boy may be manly; he
may take no mean advantages; he may play and
work and trade like a man, that is, with just and
generous respect for mutual rights; he may scorn
mean things and be shocked by sham and fraud;
he may hate coarseness, bitterness and boastful-

ness; he may abominate a lie; and be indignant
at cruelty; may loathe the profane and ribald;
may himself be the soul of honor, justice and gen-
erosity. Many a boy is a man in all but years,
and many a gray head is no man at all. It is not
years and bulk that make the man. It is not
beard, two hundred pounds and six feet in height
that make the man. It is not bone and blood and
muscle, mustached and tailor-finished, that constitute the man. Many a skeleton of a man walks
the streets, big enough and old enough, that is the
merest pigmy of a man. Half the boys in our
public schools, or who sell papers on the streets,
or black boots, are more manly than many well-
grown counterfeits of men. Nothing is truer than
that the man is not in outward things—not in
dress, position, wealth or pretension. It is not the
horse a man drives, nor the carriage he rides in,
nor the woman by his side, nor the house he lives
in, nor the servants who run at his nod for pay,
that make the man. He is more inward and out
of sight than all these. He is made up of manly
qualities, of brain and heart, of sense and sensibility, of honor, justice, fairness—made up of the
good and true things which command everybody's
respect, and which we all know and like when we
meet them. We should like them if we met them
in a tramp. We like them when we meet them
in the old or young. They are the qualities which

every man ought to have and which every youth may cultivate; and which enrich their possessor with a noble *manhood*.

This is the precious thing we have been searching for—the one more than golden wealth of worth, which these essays for young men have been driving at. Of all things rich and fair and great, nothing in this world surpasses genuine manhood. And this is the one unspeakably worthy prize which is set before the ambition of every young man. It should captivate his heart, and call forth his manliest endeavors. For this he should live. It should stimulate him in his labors, business, study, and social life. On it he should fix his hopes of success. He should believe in it and trust it to win for him the affections of the fair and the friendship of the true and good. No matter what may be his calling, a genuine manhood will serve him better than anything else. It will help the soundness of his judgment, will sharpen the acuteness of his intellect, will steady the impulses of his heart, will fortify him against temptation, will persuade him to a good life, and hold always before him the ideals of the best things for which men may live. To have a manhood, clean, pure, sincere, heartily for everything that is best and most useful, is to have the soul of what men and God most honor. This it is which will gain and keep the best friends. And friends won by such inward worth are worth having, and they will stick like brothers. Their friendship is a constant blessing and help. Oh, it is good, inexpressibly good to have the confidence and friendship of the best people!

There are people who are genuine, and many of them. They are all about us. They are not all in one church, or party. They are in all churches and parties; and some of them are not yet in any church or party, because they have not yet quite decided where they would be most at home and useful; so that young men who are true in their manhood, need have no fear of not being recognized and well known and honored in any church or party. Genuine souls will find them out. You cannot hide apple-blossoms, roses or heliotropes. Their fragrance will tell of their presence. No more can you hide true manhood. It will out. It will make the air sweet around it. It will beautify its surroundings. It will show itself in nameless ways to all about it. But it will be quickest observed and most esteemed in the churches and good associations which exist chiefly to produce and aid true manhood, so that true wisdom leads young men into these friendly organizations as their true home and place of usefulness. Everybody is stronger and better by the help of kindred spirits.

This then, true manhood, is the first and best

thing to be attained, and when attained is to be kept as sacred and guarded as the apple of the eye. Because it is so precious and rich, it is easily soiled. A little misdemeanor hurts it. A little soil tarnishes it. A slight corruption is a great injury to it. So it behooves true young men who have pride of character and a just sense of their worth, to look well to their ways, to shun evil companions and all beginnings of wrong, and hold themselves strong in the right and steadfast in every excellency of mind and life. So will they make and hold the friends they need; so will they find the profit and joy of the world's best friendliness; and so will they learn that wisdom's ways are not only ways of pleasantness, but ways of genuine and wide friendship with humanity.

CHAPTER IV.

THE YOUNG MAN AND HIS BUSINESS.

SCRIPTURE, common sense and common necessity combine to magnify the importance of business. This is a world of business, and more than almost anything else, business promotes its best interests. The difference between the savage and the civilized man is largely that one is an idler and the other a man of affairs. Idleness promotes all the things that injure men, business those that benefit them. Idleness is enervating both to body and mind and demoralizing to character; business is strengthening and elevating. Idleness is barbarous; industry manly, useful, civilizing. Indeed, civilization is the product of business. Idleness makes boobies; business makes men, men of brains, endurance and character.

So important is business that the question of what he shall do for a livelihood, is among the first a young man has to settle. The choice of vocation is about as difficult as any he has to make. With many it is the great undecided question, and they drift into maturity seeking employ-

ment at anything that may come, doing a little at
one thing and a little at another, mastering nothing and being mastered by nothing, largely wasting the years of life which ought to be training
all their powers for some special business. They
can resolve on intelligence, on virtue, on religion,
on politics, on a party and a church, easier than
a business. They can choose their friends, their
pleasures, their wives with less difficulty than
their business. It is common for young men to
be married and have children, and yet have no
business. They stand around waiting to be employed—to be somebody's servant, instead of taking hold of some business to be master of it and
forcing it to serve them and give them a place
and make them powers in the world. The wife and
family questions are important, but logically and
properly the business question comes first. Business prepares the way and provides for the wife
and family. That old proverb is a good one,
"Make your cage before you catch your bird;"
else your bird will starve, or freeze, or fly away
before you get your cage ready.

A blind boy in Illinois, had no choice of a business, but did cheerfully the only thing he could
do, which was to make brooms. So he sat down
to it with a martyr's resolution and soon became
master of his business. He persevered and after
a while employed others to help him. In a few

years he worked up a large trade, employed a
large force of help, sent his brooms all over the
country and by middle life became an important
factor in the business interests of the city where
he lived, an intelligent and respected man. He
showed the difference between drifting among all
employments and choosing one and mastering it
and putting one's whole power into it.

A young man had his eyes shot out in the late
war. He came home and not long after got awakened to the realities of the Christian religion. He
then coveted the minister's work. He went to a
blind institution and studied for a time; then to
a Divinity School and took its full course. In
due time he was ordained a minister, and now for
some ten years has been a very successful minister, happy and useful in his work as those who
have sight. This is an example of success under
difficulties, by putting one's whole force into one
calling. Still another, is the case of a blind young
man, blind from early childhod, who was educated
at the Perkins Institute for the blind in Boston,
and chose the teacher's business, who now is having
admirable success and is winning laurels for his
ability and fine character. He is the joy of all who
know him, not only on his own account, but on
account of his manly enterprise in working out a
noble career in the night-time of total blindness.
These examples of success under difficulties are

good illustrations of the importance of choosing
and mastering some special business.

This is a serious matter. Many young men find
it hard to determine what business they ought to
select. They are in doubt as to what they can do
best, or what they are best adapted to. They
know that a man who can only make a good
farmer, would better not try to be a lawyer; one
who can only trade, would better not set out for
an artist; and one who can only be a mechanic,
would better not attempt the physician. But they
do not know so well what they can do. This indecision casts many a cloud over young men's
minds, and not infrequently makes youth the
saddest period of life. Hence multitudes of young
men are adrift, not proposing anything, nor knowing what to propose. And many men go through
life and never seem to know what they are made
for, or are good for. It is a great misfortune; and
yet it is one that might be remedied by a little
resolute will. It is often the result of indecision
of character; sometimes of an ease-loving disposition; and sometimes of a fickle mind. Yet, there
are real difficulties in the way. Blind Tom, the
marvellous colored musician, much noted in his
day, a mental imbecile, almost a natural fool, who
could do but one thing, which was to make music,
at which he was a prodigy, had no difficulty of
this kind, nor had others for him. He was music

and nothing else. It captivated him, absorbed him. He hardly had to learn it. Once hearing a piece of music, he played it readily and never forgot it. So he must do the only thing he could do, or do nothing.

To do nothing should be out of the question. To be a dolittle is bad enough—a thing which everybody should abominate; but to be a donothing is just about inhuman. The donothings must be the rubbish of humanity—the miserables.

When one can do many things equally well—is "a jack at all trades," and has no especial drawing to any, and all seem equally overdone in the community, it is not easy to know what is best for him to do. But one thing may be settled at once, that in all kinds of business there seems to be no room for more, but room is being made all the time. Men are dying all the time; are retiring from business all the time; are changing business all the time; are failing, or going to other parts. This is not a stand-still world. Because a business is overdone is no reason why a young man should not adopt it, if he has a liking for it, or a way opens for him to engage in it. Nor is it any reason why one should not adopt one of several kinds of businesses, because he can do them all equally well. He cannot pursue them all successfully, so he must take one and stick to it. A division of labor is the law in civilized life. No one must at-

4

tempt everything. Choose one and go for it for all one is worth, is the true doctrine and way of success; and choose early if possible.

Now and then a young man knows exactly what he wants to do, without any reference to how much it is overdone, or neglected. It is good fortune to have such a decision ready-made. Of a family of four brothers only one knew what he wanted to do. He fixed on the prevailing business of his neighborhood, the one most overdone, and fixed on it when but a boy, and against the wishes of his parents, and against the training of his early years; and of the four he was the most fortunate in business and the best satisfied with his business life. Contented, successful and happy, the business which he made, made him, and life went well with him.

There is no room for the young in any business, if they are faint-hearted. It is for them to push in and make room. As Daniel Webster said to the young man who asked him if the legal profession was full, "There is always room up high;" so we may believe that there is always room for one who will make it. The earnest, hard-working, pushing, generally find room. Of the honorable and useful callings, the rule is to choose the one you like best and would most like to succeed in. Then master it, study it, become an adept in it, grow to it and by skill and push work it to successful results.

Don't be too covetous of an *easy* berth. The best things are not easily secured. Gold is in the *hard* rocks and usually *deep* in the mountains. The world is large and rich in raw materials and undeveloped opportunities. There are great discoveries and great inventions, and great businesses yet to be made. The field for talent, energy and industry is immense. The people never were so well off as to-day, and were never so ready to use the products of industry, taste and talent. More workers are needed every year in every department. While new fields for skill and talent are all the time being opened, the old are being renewed by improvements and inventions, so that the world is being made over constantly. Here is a great continent all about us only slighly settled and but little developed. It is crying out for population, for talent, energy, industry, to develop its resources. There is no occasion for fear, or hesitation on account of the business prospects. They are so great that no imagination can comprehend their possibilities. They are limited only by the talent and energy to be put into them. The young may take courage from the greatness of the work before them and push in for the best there is in them in all legitimate pursuits. It is of first importance that one shall want to do something *useful*. There are *hurtful* kinds of business which the evils of society produce, which should

be outlawed in the minds of all well-meaning
youth, in which they should resolve that nothing
shall induce them to engage. They should refuse
on principle not to invest money, or labor, in a
business hurtful to humanity, however financially
profitable it may be. Profits must not be weighed
against principle. Neither money, or labor, or
property must be used against the good of men.
To hurt society is not legitimate business. To
take money for that which is not "goods," is not
business, but robbery. All "goods" that come
properly under the name, are things useful to
men; and are the staple of legitimate business.
All traffic in things harmful to men is illegitimate
and not business.

Beyond the desire and purpose to engage in
some *useful* pursuit, is the ambition to make a
place in the world for one's self. Every man has
a right to an honorable place among his fellows,
to the consideration due to a man among men. It
is in the order of civilized society that this shall
be secured in legitimate business. In savage society a man secures distinction by his size, or
strength, or agility, but in civilized society by his
success in useful affairs—by his skill in work, his
industry in the useful arts, or his ability as a
manager of affairs that promote the well-being of
society. A man earns his place in earning his living. This is the recompense of well-doing. There

are few things that more help a man than these
noble ambitions, to be *useful* and to *merit and
have* the respect of his fellow-men. These stir
him to noble endeavors and hold him through his
life to do his best to act a worthy part in the great
human drama. These impulses to a worthy career are not confined to great men and great affairs,
but are equally active in men of worthy mettle in
all classes. They are a grand inspiration even in
the humble, and work the miracles of honorable
living in the great multitudes of our American
society.

A common laborer once said to Billy Gray, the
wealthiest merchant of Boston in his day, "You
needn't put on airs, Billy Gray, for I knew you
when you was only a drummer boy." "And didn't
I drum well?" responded Gray, prouder of his
drumming as a boy, than of his success as a merchant. It was the impulse to drum *well* in the
boy, that was the fountain of the good ambition
in the man. The desire to be and do well is honorable, and should possess every young man, as a
ruling passion. There is more business in this one
element of character, than in almost anything else
in men. It is difficult to make much of a man of
weak ambition. If he cares little of what others
think of him, he is deficient in one of the great
incentives to human endeavor. This desire to be
and do well is commendable. And while it stim-

ulates to business, stimulates also to worthiness of character and life.

Few men are successful in business just for the love of it. There is usually something back of it which impels to it. Sometimes it is necessity; but often a worthy ambition comes in to take the drudgery out of business toil. But when men are stimulated to business because it is the manly way of life, because it is physically and morally wholesome, because it is honorable, because it promotes all human interests, the good of society and the improvement of the world, it ceases to be simple toil and becomes life, development, manliness, the way of usefulness and happiness.

Though in choosing a business, the first rule is to choose the one you like best, it is almost certain that this will become drudgery if it is not pursued with a manly, moral purpose, for the sake of making a good character and life by it and taking a useful and honorable place in the world. We must not expect that business will be pleasure except as we put into it the great aims and uses of life. If we go about it for pleasure, or expect pleasure in it, without the aims of noble and useful living, we shall soon be corrected, for the business we think we shall like, will soon be a slave's toil. With these all business, work and toil become dignified and desirable. One of the reasons why the business of so many is fatiguing is that they put so little moral purpose and manly endeavor into it. Because they do it as a task instead of a privilege, it is a grinding tax upon them. While men work wishing for the end of the day, anxious to flee from their tasks, they will be at war with their work. They must remember that business in itself is not pleasure. It is what we carry into it that gives it pleasurable qualities.

Business is really the training school of life—the gymnasium in which power, endurance, character are developed. The mind is trained by slower processes than the body. Character matures slower than muscle. Manhood is made by the work of a life-time. Hence, when one has chosen a business, to get the best results from it, he must stick to it. He must grow to it, so that he and his business shall be almost one. He must magnify it by his best endeavors; put thought and push into it; so will it make the most of him.

The benefits of business are twofold. The first and direct benefit is support—a living, as it is called. The second is the development of character. This is the most lost sight of, yet most important. Perhaps the useful employments of men, taking all men, do more to make their characters than their schools and churches. Indeed, schools and churches are aids to the great work which human employments chiefly promote. Men, in the closely interlaced relations of society, make

life a success only when they live by the rules of
sound philosophy and true morality. These are
immensely promoted by our daily business employments.

At the bottom of a sound character and a true
life is *integrity*, and there is nothing that more
promotes it than business. Every day and every
business demands integrity. If we only work for
another we are put upon our integrity to work
honestly and well. The slave will cheat in his
work, because he works under compulsion, and
without the reward of labor. But the free worker
works as a man works, under contract, to prove
his skill and earn his reward—works to honor
himself and benefit the community.

Another element of true life is *humanity;* and
few things more promotes it than business. Business men are in constant intercourse with each
other—with the world as it is. They learn it well
—its worst and its best. They learn how to sym-
pathize with it, learn the wants of human nature
and how to be patient with it and generous to it.
Our best business men, are our best philanthropists. Such names as George Peabody, William
E. Dodge, Peter Cooper, illustrate the statement.
Few better records of charity and quick sympathy
for humanity, are ever left in this world by our
noblest men, than they left. They began life as poor
boys. They made great fortunes by faithful de-

votion to business, and were always generous contributors to charity, education and every good cause. In the last twenty years of their lives, they gave many thousands of dollars every year to good works, and were seemingly more interested in benefitting the needy classes, than in their business. As they grew rich, they grew generous and kind. And this is the proper result of business well done.

One point more should be mentioned just here. No true man is *only* a business man. He is always something more. He makes his business help him to become intelligent. Through his business he learns human nature, learns of the world, of his country and his kind, and so his interests reach out in all these directions, and he becomes broad-minded, large-hearted, many-purposed. Beyond one's business, there are always the great interests of the community, education, reform, the country, the church, demanding the care and help of business men. These great interests are best promoted by the trained judgment and interested public spirit of the men of affairs. And they are not for a few, but for all. Every man, however great or small his business, has an interest in these things as the outgrowth of business.

Then let the young men understand, that business has all the great affairs of the world in its hands. They not only furnish the money, but largely the brains to direct them. They are underneath all the grand things that promote civili-zation. Business is not selfish and narrow unless men make it so. It is not low and mean unless men carry mean spirits into it. It abounds with the grandest opportunities for great and good things; and young men should be nobly quick-ened, to go into it, not only to get a living, but to be high-minded men and make the most of them-selves and do the most for mankind that their powers will admit.

One thing more seems urgent to be said touch-ing what men shall do and how they shall do it. Though men are to "choose the business they like best," it is not wise to decide till by careful study of themselves they have determined what they are best adapted to. Their judicious friends may know them better than they know themselves. Their mental and bodily condition should do much in deciding what they shall do. Often an experi-enced phrenologist will throw great light upon this question. The science of mind is really the science of life, and if we know how to apply it in the choice and conduct of our business, our suc-cess is assured.

An expert in the study of men may so apply the teachings of this science as to make clear the kind of business to which one is best adapted and the enterprise and force he will put into it. All available light should be secured in deciding what

business we shall choose, and when it is chosen,
all our energies and our best ambitions should be
devoted to such a conduct of it as shall make our
lives useful and develop in us the best character
of which we are capable. Business is a grand
school of character, and when we are in the business to which we are exactly filled, we do best in
working out the best results both for ourselves
and others.

CHAPTER V.

BUSINESS AND SOMETHING MORE.

IN the preceding chapter, it was the aim to magnify the importance of *business*, not only as a necessity to live, but as a privilege for the development of character. It was held that business in its fullest use is a school for the acquisition of intelligence and the development of manhood. The great difference between savage and civilized life is that one is a life of idleness, and the other of business. How handless is the man of the woods! How many-handed is the man of the home, the farm, the city. This American continent as it was four hundred years ago when discovered by Columbus, and as it is to-day, shows the difference between the savage and the civilized man, and that difference shows the meaning of business. It is scarcely possible to say too much for business as an instrumentality for making men and society.

But there are qualifications to be made to all these good things said of business. There are other sides to a true life, than its business side. No man who is only a business man is a full man. It was said in the chapter on business that no true man is only a business man; he is always a business man and something more. The inquiry now is about this *something more*. So important is business, it is so magnified in community, and is so absorbing, that multitudes become mere business machines—the cogs and wheels, the belts and bolts of the world's great business factory. How many men are business men and nothing more. They can talk of nothing but business; they think of nothing but business; they do nothing but business. They are business engines, who when they are started always go off in their one direction. Like clocks which can only keep time, like scales which can only weigh, like sewing-machines which can only sew, numberless men can only do business. All their wit, all their energy, all their ambition, are trained to business. They awake from sleep to business. They have business for breakfast, dinner and supper. Their evening entertainment, and their Sunday meditation are of business; and they go to bed to dream of business through the night. They have wives and families, but they give them only the odd moments of time which necessity requires. They expect their wives to be courtesy, civility and sociability for them. They have neighbors, but they seldom see the inside of their houses, except at funerals. They have papers and books, not to read them, but because it is the fashion to have

them. The societies they join are business
men's clubs. Their holidays are fairs and business
parades. They are so full of business that they
have no time to be, or do anything else. They
see nothing in life but business. They are immense
workers and put all there is in them of talent,
worth and power into their business. They are
extremists who in this age of great business activity are caught in the swirl of material interests
without knowing how utterly they are swallowed
up, or how their one-sidedness looks to people of
a broader range of life.

This large class of men are largely lost to many
of the best interests of society, because of their
utter absorption in business. And they are los-
ing much of the best of life because they have so
narrowed their interests to the business grooves.
This is not the fault of business, but of those who
do it. Business has usurped an undue dominance
in a large number of minds, because of its necessity and importance. It is time a halt was called
to this business rush, and men were led to consider what else they should be besides "hewers of
wood and drawers of water."

Our material interests are many and important,
but we all have greater interests which it is crim-
inal to neglect. Man is a *mind* more than a body.
He is a *heart* and a *soul* more than a mind. Business relates chiefly to the body, its raiment, food,

comfort. The things of mind, heart, soul are of secondary importance in the business estimate. This is a wrong estimate which should be corrected. Every thoughtful man should reconsider this estimate; and every business man should be a thoughtful man. The purpose of this little book is in part to quicken thought in relation to human life and its well-being. To think seriously is to begin to improve. To keep on thinking is to turn life into a college. To put mind in the lead of life is to civilize, dignify and glorify both mind and life. Business has put mind and life too much into a depressing servitude. Business men are working too hard and too incessantly. Work is made a drudgery by being overdone. The business day is too long. It leaves too little time and strength for more important things. Men have minds to feed and clothe as well as bodies, and if either is to be neglected it would better be the body. Men are breaking down their bodies under the strain of business. They go to their beds every night like jaded horses to their stalls, and get up every morning feeling as worn and old as their grandfathers. Multitudes of business men are as old at fifty as they ought to be at eighty and are fuller of ailments than the doctors are of remedies. There is a nervous tension to our lives which is wrecking multitudes in the hey-day of their usefulness. Business has put on too much steam and everything else has turned to gathering fuel and firing up. The whole of the day-time and a good part of the night are put to the business rush, and many want Sunday " into the bargain." The trouble is that the material side of life is over-done. We make too much of it, and are unwise in the way of doing it. It is time to stop and think how we can do better, how we can care properly for our minds and souls and not leave our bodies uncared for.

We should begin by reducing our material wants; then shorten up the business day; then strike out for a broader and deeper intelligence.

In this line of intelligence what splendid oppor-tunities are open to us. This is the age of intel-ligence. Every known science is flourishing, and new sciences and fields of intelligence are coming often to invite our attention. Books, simple, · brilliant and powerful, are plenty as nuts in the autumn, and as easily obtained. Information the best and the richest almost floats in the air. Schools, teachers, helps to knowledge abound. Men are ignorant in our time only because they turn away from knowledge—because they re-fuse to learn—because they give the whole of their time to other things. Even men in the common walks of life in our country may be intelligent if they will. The late Elihu Burritt—

"the learned blacksmith" as he was called, became the master of fifty languages, an author, lecturer, philanthropist, the associate of scholars, the joy of the intelligent world, without neglecting his anvil and hammer. Business did not shut up his mind, did not monopolize his thoughts, or time, did not stand in the way of his attainment of knowledge, nor his growth as a scholar and a man, but helped him to all these things. He was a good blacksmith and earned a good living by his trade, earned money to buy books and help, and kept on at his business till his accumulating knowledge forced him into the world. He simply did not drown his mind in business, but fed it, kept it active, made business serve it.

The late Maria Mitchel, perhaps our country's best astronomer, who lately passed away at seventy years of age, was humbly born, and by the early death of her mother, had, when a young girl, the care of her family thrown upon her. But she did not on account of her care and work, fail to use her mind in the pursuit of knowledge. By her father's help, who had become an amateur student of astronomy, she made use of the time she could get from her work, to acquaint herself with that science, and continued its study till her scholarship made her known to the astronomical world, when about twenty-five years ago she was

5

appointed to the professorship in that science in
Vassar College. Her father was a business man
who snatched from his spare hours time enough
to make himself intelligent in astronomy and become the teacher of his afterward learned and
celebrated daughter.

These cases among many others that might be
cited prove that the noblest intellectual attainments, are within the reach of the common people
whose necessities compel them to give heed to the
affairs of business. It is true, therefore, that by
beginning young, business men may become intelligent in general scientific and practical knowledge. They may become the peers of scholars.
Their business affords them some opportunities
that scholars do not have. It gives them a world
of facts at first hand that scholars must get second
hand if at all. In the study of human nature business is the best of all schools, and the science of
human nature is the greatest of all sciences. There
is no doubt but the principal study of mankind is
man. And to whom are men more constantly
open than to the business man? Of all students
of human nature he ought to be the best. Of all
judges of men and what is for their best good he
ought to be best. As a politician, as a judge, as a
practical philosopher, he ought to surpass other
men; and he would if he did not shut himself in
so closely to business. If he read the best books,

studied history, familiarized his mind with the best ideas of practical life, entered into the great realm of intelligent life about him to possess it and be of it, he would be influential and useful in it.

Of all the practical philosophers and thinkers which America has produced, probably Benjamin Franklin heads the list, and he was a business man with only the rudiments of a common school education. But in his business and with it, he was a life-long student—a constant reader of books which gave him the best information—actively interested in everything which concerned human well-being—a seeker of intelligent society, and a searcher for new knowledge. Fortunately for him, he lived before the daily newspaper, the great dissipater of mind, the great hodge-podge of un-sorted information, in which truth and falsehood, good and evil have equal share.

Of course he who would be truly intelligent, who would enrich his mind, who would fit him-self for the best life, will read the daily newspaper but little. Books and papers which instruct, which deal with facts and principles, which are written by honest and well-meaning men, are the real helps to the information men need. These were the books which Franklin read and recommended. They are the books which will always help make men like him. In many respects he is the great pattern for business men. His life is a good one for young men to read and study. And others like his offer a great field for biographical study. Indeed, the study of the lives of the great and good is one of the most useful fields of study we can enter. There we are in the best of company, get the grandest ideas, and are quickened by the noblest ambitions. Every young man should have constantly on hand some first-class book of biography, and read a chapter every day. The biography in history is one of its most interesting and useful departments. Some histories are particularly full in this department. I know of no other so full as Macaulay's History of England, which gives a sketch of almost every leading man in the period embraced. The idea urged under this head is that every business man should be a reading man, a thinking man, a growing man in the best intelligence.

Business embraces the great body of the people and they should be intelligent outside of their business. They should know much of the world and its affairs, and may if they will. Young men who early feed their minds on useful knowledge and keep doing it, will ornament and ennoble business by and bye with a rich and helpful intelligence. They who start out to be something more than business men and put energy and industry into this resolution, will be very likely to enrich and honor their business careers.

There is another and the highest field of life from which multitudes of business men shut themselves away by their absorption in their affairs, that is, the *moral* and *religious* field. The world grows most and best by its moralities. The world is most enriched by right living. The best philosophy is righteousness in practice. The best science is the golden rule in action. The best manhood is that most charged with conscience and genuine religion. The best thing in business is its alliance with the great precepts of the gospel. All these best things are easily within the reach of all business men; and yet how many such men ignore them altogether.

There are great moral questions now agitating the minds and consciences of the best men and women of the world, questions which involve the most sacred interests of society, even business itself, which multitudes of business men think they have nothing to do with, simply because they are so absorbed with the fanaticism of business that they can see nothing else and have no interest in anything else. There are business fanatics equal to any religious fanatics—rank one-idead men, as cranky as the half-crazy advocates of the narrowest ism. They are plenty and all about us. Any business man is beside himself who neglects to ally himself with the great moral interests of society. Business is allied in interest with the

good and not with the evil of society. Business
flourishes most where there is the most right living, where moral reforms, schools, and churches are
plentiest, where people are most interested in the
best things. Business can't afford to neglect righteousness—can't afford to neglect anything which
promotes the well-being of society. Business
can't afford to join with low life, with sensualism,
with the brute inheritance in our nature and thus
put its heavy heel on morality and religion. This
is the fanaticism of wrong-headedness to which
many business men are joined. The great wrongs
in our midst are supported by such men. How
they play shy of the moral essay and lecture and
sermon. How they fight against morality in politics, against laws to promote righteousness, against
high character as a qualification for office. Surely
many business men may well reconsider their attitude toward the advancing moralities which are
the genuine promoters of all true business in their
promotion of human well-being.

This infidelity to the best things is markedly
visible in the attitude of many business men to
religion which embraces all the moralities and
humanities, all the higher interests of men. Numbers of them are simply careless of it—indifferent
to it because they are so entirely absorbed in business. They have no mind for anything else, and
think they have no time. Their notion is that

they are providers of bread and butter for the
family, and the women and children must provide the religion.   How common it is for women
to be left alone in the highest things; to be widowed where companionship is richest and sweet-
est.   How common for young men to attend their
young lady friends at church and be courteous,
and sympathetic in religious things till they are
married and a little after, and then leave them to
go widowed and lonely to the sacred opportunities they used to enjoy together.

Against this over-absorption in buisness, against
this burying the higher man in dollars and cents,
against this sinking out of sight the right and
holy life of an immortal being, and making of such
a being a mere pack-horse for the temporalities
of earth and sense, the strongest word that can be
spoken is none too strong.   It is to be hoped that
the young men to whom this word is written will
consider it well and will resolutely resolve to profit
by it.   Business is good, but there is something
more in life that is a great deal better.   There is
a great world of better things open to the manly
minds and souls of true young men.   Rise up to
these things and live for them with the devotion
of lovers to their brides.   Your business will not
suffer from, it but be improved.   There are great
numbers of the foremost business men of our
country to-day who are the foremost men in edu-

cation, reform and religion. A list of their names which could be easily gathered would be a galaxy of glory. They are all ambitious for the young men of the country to follow in their footsteps and make good their places when they are gone. None of the professions are giving better men to the world than are the business callings, proving that the high virtues that make the noblest of men, are promotive of business success. So, do your business well and read and study to become widely and wisely intelligent outside of it. Do your business well and seek to charge your life in doing it, with the high moralities which honor men in all ages and all worlds. Do your business well and give your support to every good principle that is struggling against the evil of the world and for the benefit of mankind. Do your business well, and be loyal and loving to that Great Spirit of Infinite Good Will whom we call our Father in heaven, and whose will to us and our duty to him, are shown in the perfect teachings and life of Jesus Christ.

CHAPTER VI.

THE YOUNG MAN AND HIS POLITICS.

THAT saying of Paul that " The powers that be are ordained of God," is a statement of the intention of God in human government. He has given no form of government, but he has made it clear that government is a human necessity. Men are so made that they must be governed by established rules of general application, but the form of their government is left to human politics to devise. Society could not exist without government. Social order depends on it. Safety to property and life are secured by it. All that we prize most in our civilization we owe in large degree to it. So important is it that men in the most advanced communities would soon fall back into barbarism were they not held to order, mutual respect and the support of their institutions by the strong arm of the government.

We are too little accustomed to think of what we owe to this complicated, invisible, much-maligned, yet always powerful thing which we call " the government." We complain of it, scold about it, berate its corruptions, storm at its officials, get indignant over what it does not do, and sometimes almost wish we had no government; yet it is the cherishing mother of all our most valuable institutions. We owe more to it than we can ever pay. Our homes, property and lives are secured to us by it. It fixes the boundaries of our lands, establishes and maintains our highways, aims to keep inviolable the sanctities of marriage, provides schools for our children, gives us a postal service which carries our letters to the ends of the earth and does it for the merest pittance, holds intact our town, county and state organizations, so that through them our personal rights and affairs may never be without an immediate protection, compels respect for our persons and property wherever we go in the wide world, and keeps up the commerce and intercourse of the nations so that the people of the whole world promote each other's welfare and live much as one people and one family. Government, then, in this wide view, is invaluable to us—is the support of our civilization and all our rich privileges and institutions.

Government as we have it, is the growth of all the past. It has come to us by the toil and tug and sacrifice of all the generations before us. Egypt, Persia, Greece, Rome, Judea, Gaul, Britain, Scandinavia, and all modern nations have contributed to it. It was not made, it grew. Its roots are in the soil of all people. It is the ripened fruit of the tree of humanity. The best philosophers, scholars, jurists, philanthropists, moralists, religionists, have contributed to its excellences. It is the combined wisdom of all the ages crystallized in the simple and practical forms of popular government. Imperfect as we think they are, they are the best the world has been able to give us. Their most peculiar excellence is their recognition of the equality of men before the law. They repudiate the old superstitions of king-craft and class distinctions and hail all men as equally entitled to respect and protection and equally subject to the duties of government. This which is so simple a matter to us, was the greatest innovation upon the old systems which our fathers made, and for which we have most to be thankful.

At the age of twenty-one, every young man in our country becomes the equal before the law of every other man and has a voice and hand in the administration of all public affairs. It is worthy of remembrance, that many of the most noted and influential men in the time of the Revolution and in the formation of our government were young men under forty, and some of the most brilliant under thirty. One of the youngest was Alexander Hamilton, who had no superior in power and in devotion to the American cause, who became noted as a powerful writer when but nineteen years of age. This appeal to what is best in the

young and in all the people, is one of the strong
points in our government; its most popular safeguard. It is a government by the people and for
the people and will have the support of the people
till they are terribly fallen into bad ways.

In every form of modern government it is complicated and involves many principles—is a balance of many reasons and a compromise of many
opposing forces. Not easily has this balance been
attained. It is like the adjustment of complicated machinery, the many parts and forces fitting
together in mutual relations to secure the least
friction and the greatest power and success. A
great thing, therefore, is human government in
our modern civilization. We ought to realize
what it is, how tardily and at what sacrifices it
has come to us at last, and how all our interests
are complicated with it. We cannot let it alone
because it will not let us alone. We are in its
hands and are used for its purposes; it is, therefore, for us to be purposely of it and to give it the
aid of our most intelligent direction.

It is clear, then, that in our country the young
man's *politics* is one of his great interests. All
he has or hopes for, is involved in it; and to be
indifferent to it, or ignorant of its affairs, is to be
suicidal to his own interests. And not only a *few*,
but *all* young men are called by all their interests
to an active participation in politics.

Politics is not the business of a coterie, a clique, an interested few who make a profession and a living of it only, but of all the people. It is one of the evils that has befallen the people's business that a few have monopolized it to manage it in their own interest. It is really everybody's matter, and nothing is more important than that everybody should attend with intelligence and zeal to this vital affair.

Let us look at the matter a little. *What is politics?* Webster thus defines it: "The science of government; that part of ethics which has to do with the regulation and government of a nation or a state, the preservation of its safety, peace and prosperity; the defence of its existence against foreign control or conquest, the augmentation of its strength and resources and the protection of its citizens in their rights, with the preservation and improvement of their morals." A fine definition. To consider it a little in detail may be profitable.

First. "It is the *science* of government;" not a haphazard management, not a scheme of strategy for spoils, not a game of promises and votes, not a place-hunting system of getting up in the world, but a real science, or application of known principles of human rights and duties to the conduct of public affairs, or in other words, the application of private wisdom and virtue to public life. And it is true that politics in this high sense of an ethical science, has developed some of the greatest men and grandest characters in the statesmen that have adorned the annals of countries that the world has ever known. The great statesmen always shine with peculiar lustre, both in their day and in history.

Second. "That part of ethics which has to do with the regulation and government of a nation." And what is ethics? Webster defines it, "The science of human duty." It is that which relates to morals, to rightness of conduct, to duty as applied to our social relations. Ethics in politics is morality, rightness of conduct and principles applied to public affairs. Ethics is simply another word for morality. Ethics in politics is moral principle applied in the extended relations of national life. The study of politics is the study of what is right in the conduct of a nation. And what is right in a nation is simply what is right in the individual. The moral law that should govern the individual man, is the moral law that should govern the nation. There is not one kind of morality for private life, and another for public life. Everywhere in private and in public, the golden rule and the principles of right action are to be applied to human conduct. Truly, then, politics is among the great and good things that should interest every intelligent, well-meaning person. Young and old, men and women, minis-

ters and people, scholars, moralists, every one of
public spirit, should honor and study politics, and
seek by it to apply all right principles to the well-
being of society.

Politics in a republic is actually everybody's
business, so that no common mind can be excused
from an interest in it and a duty to it.   The principles of public well-being are just as easily understood as those of private well-being.   All com-
mon-sense people understand them and ought to
resolutely seek to apply them to public interests.

Third.   The further definition of politics is,
"The preservation of the safety, peace and prosperity of the state."   This is important.   The
safety of the state must be guarded.   It is exposed to attack from without, and rebellion from
within, and its defence in either case is its loyal
people.   In the late civil strife in this country
the defenders of the national unity, were largely
young men.   It is an old saying. "Young men for
war and old men for counsel."   But while this is
generally true, it is equally true that young men
may be intelligent and wise concerning the means
of defence and the principles involved.

In the organization of our national government
there was great wisdom in many of its young
men.   None contributed more to it than some of
them.   Always in the defence of a country the
young men are a stalwart part.   But how is the

safety of our country chiefly exposed? Here is a
vital matter. We are an isolated people, and
live at a great distance from the nations that have
power to menace us. From them we are almost
perfectly safe. But are we safe from all enemies?
No, we are never entirely safe. We have enemies
within, the only ones that threaten us. They are
enemies to the manhood and virtue of young men.
Whatever deceives, weakens, unmans young men,
is the enemy of the country. Whatever impoverishes and degrades the people is the enemy of
the country. Whatever carries desolation and
woe to the home is the enemy of the country.
Whatever demoralizes society is the enemy of
the country. Have we not an institution of evil
spread far and wide among us that does all this?
What is the drinking saloon but a secret, a dire-
ful and a powerful enemy of the whole people?
Is the country safe with the saloon everywhere
working its enormous destruction of time, money,
talents and virtue? Is the country at peace with
an enemy intrenched in its midst in ten thousand
fortresses, from which it is carrying destruction
to all its great interests? Here is war all over the
country; savage, effective, perpetual. And it is
war intrenched in politics—in the degradation
and perversion of politics. Where are the defenders of the country against this enemy now? They
are chiefly the young men of uncorrupted minds

who are awake to the dangers that threaten their country. As the young men of the country stayed the tide of rebellion in '61 and by their stalwart loyalty conquered a peace that has brought great prosperity, so now may they do the same thing against any enemy, with equal loyalty and zeal. The weapons are now different, but the work is similar. It is preserving the institutions of the country and securing peace and prosperity. "Prosperity!" This is the end our definition of politics has in view, the prosperity of the people. But the saloon works destruction and not prosperity. There is no adversity more severe than saloon-wrought adversity. There is no ruin more widespread and deep-going than that wrought by the army marshalled at the call of the saloon.

But the saloon is linked with corruption, intrigue and all the powers of evil. All evil things are combined under its leadership. It is, therefore, the head and front of that great army of evil against which the genuine young men of our time and the immediate future have to fight in defence of their country. And the fight is to be on the battle-field of politics. The weapons are to be righteous principles, rational arguments, honest votes, high-toned manhood, thrown into the conflict for all they are worth.

Fourth. Our definition of politics closes thus: "The augmentation of the country's strength and

6

resources and the protection of its citizens in their
rights, with the preservation and improvement of
their morals." This is a noble conclusion which
makes politics one of the grand fields of human
endeavor.

"The augmentation of the country's strength
and resources." Where is a country's strength,
but in the righteous character of its people, the
consistency of its laws and the usefulness of its
customs and institutions? In a republic like ours,
these things constitute the great sources of power.
We are strong as we are right. In our country
no question is settled till it is settled right. Right
makes might. To stand for the right is to augment
strength. To maintain the cause of the right, to
train in the army of the right, to advocate and be
counted for the right, to vote and be consistently
zealous for the right, is to augment the strength
of the country. A country prospers in talent, in
character, in resources, in proportion as its people
live by the principles of rectitude. Rev. Thomas
Star King was once riding with an English friend
from New York to Boston. When well along in
Massachusetts the English friend remarked that
he did not see how the people raised anything on
such a soil. "Who ever heard that Massachusetts
raised anything but men?" was Mr. King's quick
reply. Men are the principal things to raise, was
his notion. Men are the important resources of a

nation, no doubt. And it is not the number of men, but the quality. And the quality depends on their intelligence, high-mindedness, loyalty to honor, duty, humanity. So politics has for its aim the production of a right-minded community. It deals with mind, character, the usefulness of life, and the things that promote them. The politics which is so conducted as to produce the best people, is the best politics. Politics is to diminish the evil and increase the good of a people. It operates against evil and for good. It is like the farmer who destroys weeds and vermin, and cultivates his good crops. Politics is national husbandry. To neglect the great farm and let it be overrun with evil growths is one of the mistakes into which politicians fall. It is resources in good and not evil that politics legitimately works for. To enrich the country in good things is the great aim.

The last point in this grand definition of politics is, "The preservation and improvement of their morals." Not simply the preservation but the improvement of their morals. Here in clear words the moral element in politics is stated. Indeed the whole definition is moral in tone. It is a bit of moral philosophy. It would have politics take hold of public life with a moral grip. And this is the great needful thing. Our public interests are abounding with great moral questions which cannot be settled except on principles of rectitude. Palliatives and compromises and evasions will not do. They demand honest, direct, righteous treatment. And the righteous settlement of many of these questions would give us a new country and a new age of the world. After all, there is no interest of the people with which politics has to do, so important as morality. Rectitude of life is the great thing. No fallacy ever stated in words is greater than that politics has nothing to do with morality. Indeed morality, right conduct among the people, obedience to all good laws and principles, is the great aim of politics. Through such conduct it aims to secure national safety, peace and prosperity.

A country like ours cannot afford to neglect the great concerns of moral life. We have a continual inflow of the ignorant and immoral elements of European society, cast upon us every year, and it behooves wise Americans to see to it that our politics shall be kept to their true uses, of benefitting the people morally as well as materially. And our young men fail in a great American duty, if they do not equip themselves with the highest wisdom and best principles of political science.

CHAPTER VII.

THE YOUNG MAN AND HIS POLITICS NO. 2.

HAVING considered Webster's definition of politics, and politics in its best and true sense, in the previous chapter, the subject will not be fully treated without considering it in its lower aspects, to which the present chapter will be given. It has come to.be the common thought that politics is corrupt and corrupting. Not a few people keep aloof from it on that account. It is offered as a reason why women should have nothing to do with it, because it is debasing. Ministers are counselled to keep aloof from it lest they fall into its contaminations. And not a few of them play shy of all political questions and actions in the fear of los-ing favor with some of their parishioners of differ-ent partisan affiliations. This is on the ground that Christian men are not manly enough to tol-erate opinions on civil matters different from their own. There is certainly a degradation of mind wrought here either in the minister, or his people, that such a thought should be entertained. It is the minister's office to teach and enforce all duties, to teach and enforce truth on all subjects involved in the practical life of men; if on the subject of politics he is restrained, there is something wrong either in politics, or the people. Literary, scholarly men and laymen devoted to religious vocations, are held from politics from fear of its evil influence. The strongest people morally are counselled not to meddle with politics lest it may hurt their characters. Only those of easy morals and uncertain character are supposed to be safe in the tainted atmosphere of political wrangling. This bad opinion of politics has certainly come to be common, and there is reason for it. There is much that passes for politics that is bad, and on this account good men have become disgusted and kept away. On this account our great lexicographer has given a second definition of politics, that is, a definition of politics in its degradation, which is this: "The management of a political party; the advancement of a candidate to office; artful, or dishonest management to secure the success of political measures; political trickery."

It is a burning disgrace that the conduct of public affairs, the management of the people's national interests, as important and dignified as falls to the lot of mortals to engage in, should ever have been so basely prostituted to personal and corrupt aims, as to justify such a definition. But such has been the fact. Politics has been and is prostituted. History is full of it. And so history is full of the fact that all good things have been prostituted to evil. Business is a good thing, but how many bad men use it for evil ends. Money is a good thing, but how fearfully it is prostituted by many whose lives are base. Marriage is a good thing, but under Mohammedanism, Mormonism, and other corrupt systems, it has been prostituted to oppression and the aggrandizement of the few. It has been made a fearful cruelty. Religion is a good thing, but nothing has been more debased to evil aims and made the occasion of more fraud, chicanery and wickedness. How fearful have been the great religious wars! We hope we have outgrown them now, but it has been a bitter experience in growing to our present just and tolerant sentiments. No wise man proposes to throw away, or be indifferent to these good things, because the evil-minded have used them for bad purposes. No more should we throw away politics because it has been misused. We must have business, money, marriage. We cannot have civilization, or good society without them. So we must have politics. It is a necessity. Public affairs must be attended to. And there must be method, order, deliberation in their conduct. This is the science of politics. And as public affairs grow large and complicated the need of talent, comprehensive judgment and business skill will be increased. In their increase will come temptation, great incentives to personal ambition and benefit, and so to the prostitution of politics. This is the rot of good fruit—the sour curd of good milk, which has come by putting weak men where strong were needed, by giving false principles the place of true ones.

A little attention to this definition of false politics will show how the falsity works to deceive. The first statement is, "The management of a political party." This goes upon the idea that men are cattle to be managed, or machines to be skilfully manipulated. It is a notion that degrades manhood. Parties are made of men, and when you say they are to be managed by politicians, you sink the men in them to a species of servitude. Soldiers are managed by their commanding officer. They are tools of their commander. His will directs them. His word is their law. They may have no opinions or plans of their own; no voice, or action of their own. They merge themselves in him—are lost in his importance. The virtue of a soldier is to be an extended and obedient part of his commander—his hand and force executing the commander's will. But how about the personal man in the subservient soldier? He is sunk out of sight, has become a nonentity. His opinions are surrendered, his will is suspended, his manhood put to sleep. His muscles and physical power are left intact to serve his commander, but no mind to serve himself. This, any one can see, is a degraded condition of the man, which is justifiable only in emergencies of public danger. It is not a natural condition to be kept as a legitimate part of civilized life. In just so much as parties become bodies of inert and obedient men, managed by accepted leaders, and led to serve their purposes, are they subversive of the liberty and dignity of manhood and the good of intelligent communities. Military necessities are usually of short duration, but politics is a constant necessity for the conduct of public affairs. In politics the individual man is the prime factor, as in business, science, philosophy, or learning. In politics each man is a thinker for himself, a student of all the questions involved. And parties are formed in politics by many men thinking alike on the questions of the hour. It is by much thinking alike that genuine and useful political parties are formed and not by non-thinking. Such parties are self-managed—that is, by mutual agreement and not by scheming leaders. Genuine parties too are changeable with the changing interests of the times, and not always the same as non-thinking would keep them. Parties are often useful for a time to destroy an old evil, or work a needed reform, but are often dangerous if they outlive the occasion of their organization. Perpetual parties are perpetual menaces to the public good, because they are liable to beget partisan interests, and pride. As a rule parties go to the bad rather than improve with age, because the pride of party is commoner than the rightness of opinion. There are more men capable of partisan pride than of sound thinking. There are more men led by partisanship than by righteous motives. Hence, the great evil in old parties comes to be partisanship. With the age of a party, partisanship is liable to rule it instead of principle, because men fall into ruts easier than into the new issues of changing time. Partisanship is afraid of new questions and ideas, clings to the old and throws the conduct of parties into the hands of leaders whose chief interest is party triumph or personal ends. In a country like this, new issues are constantly coming to the front because an enterprising people are always pushing on to something better. This calls for enterprising parties to constantly renew their life by grappling with the new things and keeping abreast of the new times.

Parties like men grow conservative with age, unless new ideas and new blood renew them. And as they grow conservative they usually grow partisan and narrow. And as they grow partisan they usually fall into the leadership of the unworthy and self-seeking.

Partisanship, therefore, is one of the things to

be dreaded in politics. Like sectarianism in religion it withers every virtue. Young men do well
to keep open eyes to this great danger and not
fall into the absurd idea that politics is the management of a political party. Give more heed to
the principles of a party than to its management.
No party is worthy without worthy principles.
No party which has been worthy continues so unless it does the worthy work of its time. Parties
must know their dangers and shun them as men
do, or they become unworthy of use.

Another part of the definition of bad politics
is, "The advancement of a candidate to office."
Among partisans the election of the candidate is
the principal thing. "Our man" as they call him,
is what they are after. They have no principles
to honor, no good of the community to serve, no
cause of right to promote, but only men to elect.
Their method is to get votes, honorably if they
can, but any way rather than not get them. This
is the method that corrupts elections, disgraces
politics, disgusts good men and cripples the country in the best things it proposes.

The further definition is, "Artful, or dishonest
management to secure the success of political
measures." The management of the party and the
election of the candidate, are of course followed
by skilful contrivances to carry measures. Here
comes in the art of demagogues, the finesse of ad-

vocates, the lobbying and trickery of partisans, the bribery of money and the pressure of base motives. This is the field of "political trickery" with which Mr. Webster closes his definition of politics in its bad use.

It is pitiable and disgraceful that such politics exists. And the worst of it all is that decent men lend themselves to it, that even good men get drawn into it by their love of their party. There is an infatuation in politics, its cliques, its promises, its honors, that lead men into strange relations and actions.

Young men ought to know all these dangers and be prepared by their knowledge, to resist them. And they should know too that this is a great field in which adroit, cunning, and talented men play their games of personal greed and ambition. Knaves and rascals are here with oily tongues and wily manners to deceive the very elect, with the base multitudes of the ignorant and grovelling to serve their purposes. Surely this side of politics has a forbidding aspect. It is a foul pit. And yet we must have politics. It is one of the necessities of republican civilization. It has in hand the great affairs of the country—even the great American republic, which if wisely conducted is likely to grow to embrace the continent; the birth and freedom of which cost treasures of patriot money and blood. Read the story of colo-

nial oppression and wrong suffered by our fore-
fathers at the hands of   tyrant king and venal
parliament.   Read of their patient sufferings for
years, of their commerce restricted, their manufac-
tures prohibited, their representation denied, their
laws vetoed, their petitions spurned, their growth
prevented, their success thwarted to keep them in
colonial dependence—one of the worst cases of
bad politics on record.   Then read the story of
their healthy growth, their wisdom, courage, loyalty, their announcement of great principles, their
puritan morality, their public spirit, their devout
trust in Providence and faithful love of English
law and liberty.   From 1761 to 1783, the history
of the American colonies is richer in great principles, men and deeds, than any other portion of
purely human history.   It is of marvellous interest.   It reads like chapters from some divine trag-
edy.   The contrast between England and her colonies, between the mother and her daughters, is
so marked that the mother seems robed in black
and the daughters in white.   This is a portion of
our history that all American young men should
be familiar with.   Its characters are among the
finest in the world.   James Otis, Samuel and John
Adams, Joseph Warren, John Hancock, John
Dickinson, Benjamin Franklin, Thomas Jefferson,
George Clinton, Patrick Henry, George Washington and many more, have left records of charac-

ters and lives that will only grow more luminous
with the passing of the ages. They stand among
the noblest of their kind, great, broad-minded,
true-hearted, strong-headed men, the story of whose
greatness and nobility should be familiar to every
American youth. The birth-throes of this nation
ought to throb in every young heart. We are
only a century from those great times, and yet
many of our youth scarcely ever read of them—
know of them only as the misty things of the past.
It is amazing to see how those men understood
what they were doing—foresaw the greatness of
the work they had in hand—and knew how out of
the great nation they were founding, the whole
world was to get liberty, law and blessing. They
often in their great flights of speech, picture the
world as we now see it—all nations lighting their
torches of knowledge and political life at our
flame.

This great country which cost so much, which
is so much, which promises to be so much more,
and which is the outgrowth of righteous and enduring principles, is soon to come into the hands
of its youth. Its homes, its business, its property,
schools, churches, governments, politics, and institutions, are all to become the possession of those
whose minds are just opening to these great realities. What will they do with this magnificent
patrimony? Will they keep it up to its high tide

of growing excellencies, or will they by their incompetency and unfaithfulness let it down into the mire of greed and lust where so many nations have gone to ruin? Shall the grand things secured to us by the great men of the past century, be corrupted and lost by the small men of this, or shall the rising young men see their opportunity and rise to it to make of their country a still grander field for the enterprise and life of a great people? .

Our young men ought to be politicians. Whatever else they are, their country is of first interest to them. It gives tone and character to everything else. Home, business, profession, all interests take much of their value from the laws, politics, government of the country. They should remember that this is the people's country. We have no ruling class. The people make and unmake their rulers—make and unmake their laws. The people through their chosen servants conduct all public affairs. It is for the people—all the people to be acquainted with the essential principles of our laws and the administration of our government, and to see to it that the great public interests are wisely and faithfully conducted. Gov. Gage of Massachusetts, King George's governor before the Revolution, complained to the parliament that there was no managing a people when every man in the community studied law. That, he said, was the case in Massachusetts. The

fact was that almost every man knew his rights
as a British subject. The whole people were
studying their rights. They became political econ-
omists—a community of practical philosophers.
What John Adams said on the day of the declaration of independence, was literally true, "Britain
has been filled with folly, America with wisdom."
These were what gave us our independence, our
republic, our grand institutions, the folly of Britain and the wisdom of America. If true, what a
grand saying. And it was true. It was the wisdom of great intelligence and moral worth. That
is the wisdom we need now—the wisdom a republic always needs, the wisdom of an intelligent and
virtuous people. It is the purpose of our common
schools, to carry education to all the people that
they may be kings and queens in the sense of
ruling themselves through the instrumentality of
republican governments.

Let our young men become wise in the principles of human justice and rights before the law,
the principles of honest statecraft, of righteous
voting and legislation, of the high practical and
moral uses of the government, and they will see to
it that the government suffers no detriment at
their hands. It is vastly important that the young
men understand their duty to their country and
have the moral force to carry it into practical service. If they do not, its great interests will suffer

from their incapacity. The country cannot take care of itself. They must do it, or it will not be done. The present actors will soon be gone. It is the young men of to-day, or nobody, that will carry on these great affairs. The government is but a machine—a method of serving its people, and will always be what they make it. Let it increase in efficiency by the continued increase of the wisdom and virtue of its people.

7

CHAPTER VIII.

THE YOUNG MAN AND HIS MONEY.

" THE love of Money is the root of all evil," was said by the Great Teacher. The force of this teaching went against money as a dangerous thing; for it was easy to carry the stress of the teaching over from the *love* of money to *money* itself, and so call money the root of all evil. The point in the teaching is against the *love* of money. Money is left in its innocence, as harmless in itself as a buttercup, or a diamond. It is only in the bad uses to which men put it that it ever becomes evil. In modern times there has come another saying which men like better—" Money makes the mare go," the meaning of which is, that money is a motive power of great force among men—a dominant power. The two statements are not so different as they seem. They are only different ways of setting forth a fact important for everybody to know, that money is so potent an agency in this world that it has a controlling influence in its affairs. Go into the busy marts of business—into the industries of men along the thoroughfares of

exchange and travel, into the offices of the professions, the halls of learning, the churches, the
courts, the headquarters of official power, and
everywhere it will be seen that money represents
and serves all these important agencies. Go
among the evil things that annoy and disgrace ·
men—the things that corrupt society, ruin nations
and make hard and wretched the ways of humanity, and money is there equally the great agency
in promoting the evil of the world. It seems to
be true that money moves the world, simply because it is the representative of all values, real, or
fictitious.

It is apparent at once that money has no moral
quality—is neither good nor bad. Neither the
money itself nor the love of it is the root of evil
only as it is coveted and used for evil purposes.
The evil is not in the money but in the one who
covets, or uses it. It is an innocent and very con-
venient agency for the expression of values in aid
of exchanges between men.

Money must be called an invention. There is
but little intrinsic worth in it. It is nearly use-
less except for the purposes of traffic; and yet by
the invention of men, it has been made one of the
most serviceable utilities of our civilization. It is
good in itself and is to be sought in just and honorable ways; and sought earnestly and with perseverance. If it has any moral value it is in its

use, and not in itself.   The same dollar can be
used for charity, or cruelty, for religion, or sin.
The money that yesterday served an outlaw, may
to-day serve a saint.   Moral character is not in
money but in the one who uses it.   A case illus-
trative of this is in the history of the struggle of
the people of the United States for their independence.   In that struggle there was one very
brilliant and for a while useful young man who
served the cause with much efficiency till his name
became a tower of strength, and he was promoted
to giddy heights of honor; and yet in a brief time
thereafter, he blackened that name with deepest
disgrace and associated it forever in this country
with Judas Iscariot.   This was Benedict Arnold,
who attempted to sell his country for a price—
Arnold, the traitor.   He seemed as self-sacrificing,
honest and zealous for the cause he had espoused,
as the great patriots of the day; had the confidence of Washington, the army and country; and
yet leaped from his high position into the infamy
of a traitor.   And why did he do it?   Because he
did not know the value and use of money.   He
was trusted with important duties with his headquarters in Philadelphia.   The glitter of military
and fashionable life was about him.   Society
courted and flattered him.   He lived high and fast;
and in a short time got into debt—heavily in debt.
He could not raise the money to pay, and was

looking disgrace in the face. Soon after he was transferred to West Point, near the headquarters of the British in New York. The British officers had money to buy those they could not conquer in the field. Arnold's debts and their ready money made the temptation too great for him, and he sold himself to them to pay the debts his foolish vanity had contracted. He bargained to sell his command, it was believed, but the plot was discovered in season to save the command, while he fled to the enemy—a perpetual monument of financial incompetency.

It is one of those cases which occur so often, where life is ruined by a failure to understand the *moral* uses of money. It is true that money has moral as well as material relations and involves *character* as well as comfort and show.

The same history that gives us Arnold's infamy. gives us the story of Benjamin Franklin's noble services to his country and the cause of popular government. In detailing the elements of his great character, his rigid *economy*, practiced through all his life, at kings' courts, as well as in humble stations, is spoken of to his credit, as giving beauty and strength to the republican simplicity of his life. This is said of him, that "he practised economy that he might be *independent*." To be independent of monied obligations which one cannot meet, and all the embarrassments and anxieties which come with them, puts one in a position to make the best of himself. The poor debtor enmeshed in obligations is like the fly entrapped in the web of the spider. The more he struggles the more he is bound and the more he wastes his strength in vain.

Franklin's maxims of practical life, so simple, wise and moral, that everybody at once sees their excellence, gained him the title of philosopher. And putting his own maxims into practice made him one of the greatest as well as worthiest of the great men of the world.

Here are two men of marked ability and commanding positions before the world, committed to a great cause, each able to do grand things for his country and mankind and build his own fame higher than the stars; in a new country, poor and struggling for an existence, and for the equal rights of all its people; its soldiers half-fed, half-clothed and half-paid; the most of its people suffering great deprivations to secure nationality and freedom; one of them depriving himself of all luxuries and limiting his expenses to actual necessities, though serving his country in foreign courts; the other using lavishly all the best things he could get and piling up debts in the presence of his famishing soldiers. A sharper contrast can scarcely be found between two great men serving a great cause. And the contrast is chiefly in the very matter which this chapter is urging young men to consider as vitally important, which is the right use of money. By having false ideas on this subject, Arnold went to ruin and made the foulest blot on our revolutionary history. By having right ideas and practices on it, Franklin became one of America's noblest men and one of the world's greatest philosophers. Such men are ex· amples for young men to study, one as a warning, the other as a guide.

When young men are well along in the evening snadows of a long life, they will have learned that the practical questions of money and its uses, are among the very real and important ones needful to be well settled in every-day life. And they will find too that their early settlement is a good part of success. A failure here is a failure almost everywhere. The unfinancial man usually fails in his intellectual and moral purposes as he does in practical affairs. No young man has any right to be a spendthrift in his young days and expect to become a financier and wise user of money after that. Prodigality, improvidence, carelessness of money obligations, are seldom effectually repented of. As a man begins in these things, he is very likely to continue. As the boy begins with the use of pennies, the man is likely to continue with the use of dollars. The lesson early learned in the use of money is not readily forgotten. Neither

becoming very rich nor very poor is apt to change
this matter.

Everybody finds poverty an uncomfortable companion to live with. Whether in the kitchen,
parlor, or out in the world, it is disagreeable. The
old saying that "Poverty is no disgrace, but it is
mighty inconvenient," is accepted as true by all
the unfinancial. But is it true? In most cases in
this country poverty is the result of evil habits, or
indolence, or carelessness in the use of money,
which a right sense of moral obligation might
have corrected. As a rule, poverty is a disgrace.
Americans ought to be ashamed of being poor except in cases of misfortune. Take any ten healthy
boys in the community, a portion of them will be
poor, and some of them will be well off. Why
this difference, except that some are careful in
the use of money, and some are not? In most
cases there is blame in being poor. Those who
are not poor make the necessary sacrifices to become financially independent. Good financial conditions are attainable as are good intellectual, or
moral conditions. Poverty must be classed with
ignorance and wickedness as an evil to be overcome by the needful efforts and sacrifices. And
those who do not make the necessary efforts and
sacrifices are to be blamed for their poverty as for
their ignorance, or wickedness. There is a mawk-
ish sentiment in relation to poverty as there is in

relation to drunkenness, as though the poor and
the drunken are to be pitied more than blamed, to
be condoned rather than punished. Sometimes
they are, and so are all sinners. When misfortunes rather than faults have been the occasions,
pity and pardon come in to do their work of
mercy. On all just principles of philosophy and
morality men are to be held responsible for their
poverty. There are three words that express the
conditions of financial competency; they are industry, economy and perseverance. Industry keeps
one at the work of earning, accumulating money;
economy saves it, makes it self-accumulating, in-
terest-bearing, profit-earning; perseverance holds
one steadily, all days, and all years, to the earning
and economizing work. The three acting together
almost invariably overcome poverty.

The great majority of American men are not
poor. They have secured their competency by
their own efforts and sacrifices. They have earned;
made their earnings earn, and kept on doing it.
In this work they have made themselves and their
country what they are. The vast accumulations
of property in our farms, homes, shops, mills, highways, railroads, telegraphs, telephones, cities, institutions and industries, over the whole area of
this young country, are the products of the earnings of the thrifty who have fought poverty face
to face and conquered it. This property has not

come by luck but by pluck. It has not come by
idleness and wasting, but by work and economy.
It has not come by going to bed every night as
poor as in the morning, or getting up every morning as poor as the night before. Men have earned
and saved and money has been accumulated. And
it has all been done little by little. It has all been
earned and saved penny by penny, just as we must
all earn our money if we have any. Money does
not come in mountains but in molehills. As the
rivers come from springs, so do the great estates
from the little earnings.

One of the great troubles with young men is
that they have not learned the power of pennies.
They think of rich men as having got their riches
in great sums, rather than penny by penny. They
think it is small business to earn and save money
by the penny. They waste freely and save with
reluctance their pennies. They do not believe in
resisting poverty with pennies. They see no riches
in pennies. They are the poor man's money. But
really, the light estimate of pennies keeps many a
man poor.

Money is one of the great instrumentalities in
the conduct of the affairs of this world; and on
this account it is more likely than any other, to
be perverted to evil uses. We have had in this
country two great illustrations of the power of
money for evil. One of them is now happily in

the past. They are slavery and intemperance. Slavery for many years dominated this country— dictated its presidents, its congress and its judiciary, as well as its domestic and foreign policies.

It was king in Republican America. How did it get and hold this power? By the money there was in it, or supposed to be in it. It was only when moral and patriotic considerations rose above mercenary ones that this evil power was destroyed. Now it has become clear to all that the supposed wealth-power in slavery was fictitious—that it was really a poverty-engendering institution and was making the nation poor instead of rich, especially that portion of it where it existed. Its riches wrung from the toil of unpaid labor, went into the hands of a scattered few, who not having earned it, knew not how to use it, nor the principles of domestic and social economy by which families and communities thrive. The most that could be said for slavery in its palmiest days, was that it made a few rich, while the many remained in hopeless poverty, the slave in degraded servitude, and the section of country where it existed, in a general paralysis. This perversion of the money power was a mighty evil, reaching every interest in individual and social life.

Intemperance, or the liquor traffic, now holds a similar position in our country. It dictates our politics, officials and legislative action. Repub-

lican America is on its knees again to a monied
power. The money in the liquor traffic is its chief
source of power. It controls votes, legislation,
judiciaries, politics, because it controls money.
But like slavery, it accumulates money in the
hands of a few; and like slavery it impoverishes
the many to enrich the few, takes the earnings of
hard-worked labor without giving an equivalent
and leaves its defrauded victims in a miserable
servitude to vice and poverty. Like slavery it is
a breeder of poverty. It produces nothing good,
but immense evils. Those into whose hands it
carries money are incompetent to its legitimate
uses to benefit and build up society, because of
the moral perversity that comes to them with its
accumulation. Perverted money works perversion of mind and conscience. Stolen money has a
curse upon it. Liquor-filched money has a worse
curse upon it, for the woe and crime and sin it
produces are chargeable to it. No evil in our
community is at all to be compared to the liquor
traffic and use sustained chiefly by perverted
money.

The fearfulness of the two great evils referred
to ought to put every young man upon his guard
against coveting money gained in any false or
crooked way. Such money is "blood-money."
It is cursed in the getting. It is not money gained
anyhow that we have any right to want, or that

will do us any good. It is clean money that will serve us well. Money that stands for fraud, oppression, or fellow-suffering, is to be held as the price of crime. Such money is to be spurned, rather than accepted on any conditions.

The honorable pursuits of society are all arranged upon the idea of mutual helpfulness. They open to us the sources of independence and plenty. In them we should find employment for our energies. The useful employments give useful money, the hurtful employments hurtful money.

Money is good for us in part because it is good for us to earn it. The value of it is in earning it. To pick it up as we can gravel in the river bed, is not to find it useful. It must be honestly earned to render us good service. Suppose a young man can play a shrewd game of cards at the gaming table and make a fortune, shall he do it? *No*, a thousand times *no!* Why? Because it is not a legitimate business; because it robs others to get it himself; because it is the business of gamesters and robbers, and not of honest men; because such money is corrupted in the getting and its possession is a moral debasement. It is mean, even to covet money in such a way. There is character to be made in making money. There is virtue and noble manhood in the right style of money-making. Out upon money corrupted in the getting. Abominate the money made in ruining humanity.

Another point should be noted. It is not the great fortunes that we need, but the means to meet our reasonable wants—enough to give independence of want and misfortune—competency. There is moral danger in great riches. The temptation to pride in great gains, to covetousness, to arrogance, to indifference, to human striving and need, to hardness of heart, is great. The temptation too, to live for money, as the miser does, or to become the servant of money as many rich men do, is great.

The true notion of business and money-getting, is to be so employed as to live independent of others' help and make our business and money, as well as ourselves, helpful to others. Money-getting should not be thought of as a selfish scramble, but as a useful employment, not less beneficial to the world than to ourselves.

We should begin early to act upon the right ideas of money and money-getting, that we may be trained to self-help and the activities and virtues which give us judgment, industry, economy and integrity.

It is manly to set one's self bravely about the affairs of the world in some honorable calling, with a view to being an independent actor among men. It is manly to cultivate the qualities which make a successful man in the conduct of the business side of life. It will be found at last that success

even in virtue and religion, will be found to have
a very practical basis. A full man, like a diamond, is many-sided, and must be right all round,
and many of the sides are ground to their best re
flection in the good conduct of business affairs.

CHAPTER IX.

THE YOUNG MAN AND HIS TIME.

"Time is money" is an old saying. But this only begins to tell the truth. Time is more than money. It is learning, wisdom, character, success, power, when put to its right uses. Time makes the men who fill the ages with worth, the institutions that enrich the world, the epochs that glorify history. All great things are the product of time. Longfellow has written a volume of practical wisdom in one line:

"Learn to labor and to wait."

Time is the element of labor which gives it success. The efficiency of labor is in stroke after stroke long continued. "A continual dropping wears a stone." It is not only the dropping but its continuance that does the wearing. It is not only labor but its continuance that works success. Spurts of labor, spasmodic smartness, lightning flashes of work are not enough. It is the spurt kept up, the smartness long drawn out, the lightning made perpetual, that accomplishes creditable things. Minutes are little things and small in their results, but minutes held to good uses till they make hours, and hours held on to till they grow into years, and the years made fruitful till they ripen into ages, accomplish the great things in human history.

A few years ago some one started a complaint against our American colleges that they failed to make great men as did the old colleges. And all the papers took it up and a ringing complaint went the rounds that our colleges had degenerated because they produced no more giants. But after all the papers had become hoarse with their growling, some considerate editor thoughtfully said, "Gentlemen, you are too soon with your complaints. Colleges are to prepare men to grow and do; but no men are heard from as great men in any broad, national sense, till they have been out of college, at least twenty-five years; after that they mature into greatness and become widely known." Then he cited the few truly great men of the present century in this country and Europe, noted when they left college and when they attained greatness in any generally accepted sense, and showed that *time* was a very important factor in the development of greatness.

But Longfellow's gem of wisdom asks us to *wait* as well as labor, that is, wait while we labor. There is *time* spent in waiting, not time spent in idleness, but in labor. We must labor without

8

expecting immediate results. The results of labor are slow in coming. Seeds are slow in germinating and slow in their early growths.

This lesson of the value and true importance of time in the make-up of our lives and successes, is one of the most difficult for the young to learn. Youth is the ardent season. It is full of fire and zeal. Its imagination is active. It does not want to wait. It is in hot haste for action and attainment. It tires of old-fogy slowness, and covets quick returns and striking results in every enterprise. Yet the old law holds good that time will have its slow way in all its great results.

All the short cuts to greatness are accidental and not legitimate. They are not to be copied, or to be cited as examples. There are some cases of quick success that have the appearance of being secured by some smartness, or short-hand skill, but examine them closely and they usually prove the old law that time will have its slow hand on all truly great and good results. The cases of success by lottery luck, are mere chance affairs and illustrate no law, or principle. There is the case of Charlotte Brontë, who while yet a poor young woman, even a poor, timid, country girl, who had never been but a little way from her father's rural home, had never worn anything better than a gingham dress, who woke one morning to find herself great, to find all London, yea, all the great

men and women of England half-crazy over her
and her work, and all in a hot dispute as to
whether she was a man or woman, as to whether
she was some well-known author under a *nom de
plume*, or some new star come with a flash into
the zenith of the literary firmament. She had
written *Jane Eyre* and after offering the work to
the most of the noted publishers of London and
having it refused, she at length found one, Mr.
Campbell, an obscure publisher, who would ven-
ture on the dangerous experiment of publishing
the work of an unknown author. She had written
under the name of Currer Bell. The publisher
had addressed his letters to Mr. Currer Bell, and
they had been answered by Currer Bell. He had
no reason to think anything else only that the
author of Jane Eyre was a man. But some of
the women readers thought they saw the touches
of a woman's hand not likely to have been written
by a man. But still the general thought was that
Currer Bell was a man, and the literary magnates
soon insisted that he must come to London to give
them the pleasure of his acquaintance. They
must know so great an author and he must be
admitted to their circle of honor. Mr. Campbell
pressed Mr. Bell to come to London, accept the
hospitalities of his home, and give the literati of
the great metropolis the pleasure of his acquaintance. So the arrangement was made. Miss Brontë

went to great, frightful London and was taken by the stage to Mr. Campbell's door. She rang the bell and was ushered into the waiting-room with her heart almost in her mouth. Soon a gentleman came in and introduced himself as Mr. Campbell, "and I am Currer Bell," she replied. He was astonished beyond measure, but, too much of a gentleman to be utterly overcome, he made the best he could of his embarrassment; brought in his wife and family and was soon on easy terms with her. The great men were astonished, but all came with their hats in their hands to pay their respects to the genius which had produced Jane Eyre—even the great, burly, bearish Carlyle came and was tame and docile and complimentary.

This sudden popular triumph, one of the greatest ever produced by any author, had the appearance of falsifying the common law that greatness and success are attained only by long-continued efforts. But Miss Brontë's history makes her one of the most rigid illustrations of the law. She had sacrificed her childhood and youth to study reading, meditation and writing. She had struggled and suffered so much that she was prematurely matured in soul life. She had wrestled with all the great questions of the time, theological, moral, social, political. Her inner life was a furnace of great fires of mind, heart and conscience. With her mother dead, her father a sort of anchorite clergyman, shut up in his study, with three younger sisters intellectual, conscientious, morbid like herself, all given to introspection and writing their thoughts for each other; a brother who went to bad habits and broke his sisters' hearts; she had mused, read, thought, and written and suffered, till she had a vigorous, positive, incisive, original and brilliant mind that had its own views of life and all its great questions, and its own sharp and powerful ways of discussing them. She had written several books which had not then been published. She and her sisters had some years before published a little volume of their early poems, but they had not then been much read and had not brought them from their obscurity. So it was true of her that she had labored and waited for the power to write Jane Eyre.

It is always true then that *time* is one of the essential and important elements that enters into the make-up of strong mind, mature judgment, worthy character and notable success.

2. It is an old and true saying that "whatever is worth doing at all is worth doing well." Now it is equally true that nothing can be done well without giving the proper amount of time to it. As a young man would you learn a trade, or a business, or a profession by which to earn your living, in which to work out a reputable character, and make a useful career in the world? Would you

hurry so important a matter as that? cut it short
in its ripening time, and thus cheat yourself of
the complete preparation, just to save a little
time? How common is this suicidal practice. How
common for young men to think that they have
not time enough to learn a trade, or study a profession well, and so cheat themselves of the very
power to succeed. Now more than formerly is
ample preparation a necessity. Time and money
and effort put into the preparation, are invest-
ments which usually pay the best dividends.
Once men could start in any of the professions and
work out a kind of success by dint of cheek and
push, because professional men were few, and the
people but little informed in such matters; but now
the professions are full and well equipped, and those
who would succeed in them must do it largely by
an efficient preparation. The day is over for half-
lawyers, half-doctors, half-clergymen, or half-me-
chanics, farmers, or business men, to make any
marked success. This is the day of *skilled* labor,
of *intelligent* professional service. The half-pre-
pared men are cheats. They cheat themselves and
employers. It is common for young men to feel
that they have not time enough for a complete
educational outfit for a profession, and so they
take some short cut to a profession, either by
taking some easy course in college and beginning
professional studies, or keeping from college al-

together. They get but a smattering of the things they do study, some half-knowledge, and with it some half-development of mind and habits of half-investigation which go with them through life. They get minds full of fog which are in danger of never clearing up to clear perceptions. Thus half-equipped for any place or calling, they go lame and hobbling on to the far-off end, learning when it is too late, to regret their mistake in not taking the hardest and fullest course of preparatory study.

It is getting to be very common for large boys not contemplating a profession, to skip from the high school to some penny-catching employment, and thus go into business life with the merest smattering of an education, to be sham men ashamed of their ignorance all along their careers. They fancy that they are short of *time*, when they have all the time allotted to anybody. This dodging the high school is the merest boy's play. There is nothing manly, or sensible in it. The wisdom of the past has given the American boys the high school as the people's college. It is adapted to the minds and needs of the people to prepare them for citizenship, business, and life's common cares and responsibilities. It is for all the boys and it is cruelty to themselves and the country for them to fail to use it for the most it can possibly be worth to them. For the honor of America, for the good of the boys that are to be men, let them be held to the full benefits of the high schools! There is time enough after the high school, for a grand and successful life, especially if no time is wasted.

They who *waste* no time are seldom short of time to do everything well which needs to be done at all. Wasted time is the bane of many a life. It is this more than anything else that cuts short preparatory education. Time trifled away, time idled away, time fooled away is what deprives many a life of success and fills it with shame. This is a point of vast moment to many a young man. The love of fun and frolic, the craving for society, the passion for a good time, so overcome many young men of good abilities and intentions, as to dissipate their force of character and cripple every energy for any great purposes, or noteworthy pursuits. Their waste of time will make them perpetual weaklings.

Sir John Lubbock says, "Time is often said to fly; but it is not so much the time that flies; as we that waste it, and wasted time is worse than no time at all."

"I wasted time," says Shakespeare, "and now doth time waste me."

Lord Chesterfield says, "Every moment you now lose is so much character and advantage lost; as on the other hand, every moment you now employ usefully, is so much time wisely laid out at prodigious interest." Dante says:

"For who knows most, him loss of time most grieves."

And Faust,

"Are you in earnest ? seize this very minute,
What you can do, or think you can, begin it."

This leads directly to the value of *evenings*.
The evening time from six to ten o'clock does more
of help or harm to young men than any other
time of the same length. If you know how a
young man spends his evenings, you can predict
with tolerable certainty the style of life he will
live and the degree of his success. The four
evening hours of each day ruin more young men
than all the other time of their lives. They are
the hours for gossiping, riding, idling, dissipating
time and mind, drinking, gambling, smoking and
all vicious things. They are not only the waste
hours, but the wicked hours, in a vast number of
young lives. They are the dark hours, poison
hours, dreadful hours to very many. They are
the hours that make vagabonds, spendthrifts,
drunkards, criminals, that fill our lock-ups, jails,
prisons, that torture parents and rob homes.

On the other hand, they are precious hours for
those who will use them well. Four evening hours
of each day, give twenty-four hours each week—
two full days of twelve hours each, which devoted
to study or personal improvement, give time
enough to master the study of mechanics, archi-

tecture, civil engineering, drawing, metallurgy, short-hand reporting, telegraphy, type-writing, medicine, law, or theology; or pursue any special or full course of college studies; or to read all the science, history, or literature any one has need to read to be master of any branch of scholarship or reading. In proof of this may be cited the case of Elihu Burritt, the learned blacksmith. In the early part of his life he began the study of the ancient languages after his full day's work at his trade and at the great disadvantage of having no teacher. He pursued his evening studies as faithfully as his day work, and they became his pastime and pleasure in a little while. By the time he was fifty he was intelligently familiar with about as many languages as he was years old, and was probably one of the best linguists of our country. He was an independent, successful blacksmith by day, and a critical, enthusiastic linguist by lamplight. This evening study made the last twenty-five years of his life rich in literary treasures and gave him the acquaintance of scholars in all parts of the world. He became a noted author and philanthropist honored as much for his worth as [a man, as for his wide scholarship. If he had spent his evenings as most blacksmiths do, he would not have been known out of his neighborhood, nor have served the world in any of its great interests. His evenings made him a great and useful man and put his name among the honored of his kind.

Another example, equally noted is forced upon us by the excellency of his life and the marked success that attended all he did. It is that of Peter Cooper who died a few years ago in New York City at the ripe age of ninety-three, as much honored in the hearts of the American people as any man of his time. From one sketch of his life the following is cited as illustrating the point in hand:

"Thus deprived of even the meagre opportunities of an education then existing, at the age of seventeen he was apprenticed to coach-making in New York City, at which he continued for four years. This period indicated those germinal traits that grew into such grandeur and fruitfulness. His force of character displayed itself in his re sistance of those nightly attractions and seductions of the city, and devoting his evenings to useful reading and experimenting. With rare wisdom for a country youth, he valued the evening hours and utilized them to supply his deficiency of education and to train his mental powers for manly strife. In this he set his first example to young men. The critical hours of the workingman are those between sunset and slumber; they determine his character and destiny, his victory or defeat. In these hours have been wrought some of the grandest characters on record. Franklin the printer, Linnæus the shoemaker, Stephenson the miner, Hugh Miller the stone mason, when the day was done, consecrated their evenings to study and experiment, and the result was Franklin the scientist and statesman, Linnæus the botanist, Stephenson the inventor, and Hugh Miller the geologist. Mr. Cooper, when other young men were in the saloon, or the theatre, was training his mind for those enterprises which have proved most useful to himself and beneficial to mankind.

The first practical result of these evening studies was his invention of a machine for mortising hubs; and his employer being so pleased with him, offered to build him a shop and establish him in the business. This he declined, having a wholesome horror of debt, again evincing his force of character and self-reliance." This is enough for the present purpose. It is not needful to follow the grand career of success and usefulness, growing out of his wise use of his evening hours and all his time and powers; but it was one of the finest wrought out by the best men of this world—a career of steadily developing character, usefulness and fame. He became great, wealthy and good, and grew more and more so all the days of his long life. The evening hours, the off-times, as well as all times were made to serve him.

This is the conclusion of this whole matter that

their use of time makes men. If they use it well
their lives are successful; if they put it to ill uses
they are failures. It is vastly important that men
learn this great fact early and resolve to use their
time to the best advantage. Not great powers
so much as good sense in their use, gives men
success.

CHAPTER X.

THE YOUNG MAN AND HIS HABITS.

It has been said that "Men are creatures of habit." It has passed into a proverb that "Habit is second nature." These sayings indicate a tendency in us to contract habits. Perhaps habit may be called the state of action into which we educate ourselves. Certain it is that habit is an attained state. We are not born with habits; we do not buy them, or borrow them. They are not natural to us. They are not the results of instinct. The robin always builds its nest the same way; all robins do. Take a young robin from its nest before its eyes are open, and bring it up by hand, without its ever seeing a robin's nest, and when it wants a nest it will build it in the robin's style of architecture, and will build the first time as good a nest as ever after. This is instinct. What instinct is, or how it operates, no one can tell. Other birds have other ways of building which they seem to know without learning. The beaver is a house-builder, but builds unlike any other animal, and builds always on the plan of his people, and without knowing how. He does it by instinct. The bee lives a short life, under the established government of the bee community, builds a house, fills it with bread and honey, which nothing else living knows how to make, and does everything in his busy, brief life by instinct, having never learned how. The spider is one of the brightest creatures we have about us—a born spinner, and a born house-builder, and a born trapper, and yet his life is lived almost wholly by instinct. And yet instinct is a miracle-worker to us human creatures. We know nothing about it and can learn nothing about it. It seems to be an inward voice, or inclination, or power, that directs what to do, and how to do it, without premeditation, or study. But habit is not instinct, nor does instinct have anything to do in its formation. Instinct is bright, but habit is dull, slow to learn and slower still to unlearn. Thick-headed habit has to do a thing many times before it knows how to do it; and when it learns how, goes on stolidly doing the same thing, good or bad, hurtful or helpful, in unteachable obstinacy. Perhaps it may be said that habit is the dullard's education. It is what he has attained by long drill. It is not attained by any forecast, intuition, or brightness, but only by round-and-round plodding. Habit is the opposite extreme from instinct. It is a slowly educated, or made condition of action. It does not come suddenly, or even in a brief time, but slowly. It takes *time* to make habits, and not much else. But little mind is required; but little common sense; but little heart. Usually the less strength of mind, the more strength of habit. And usually too, habit increases as virtue diminishes. The weaker the man the stouter the habit, is the rule. Thought and virtue enter but little into habit.

It is true that many men of mind form very strong habits; but they do it in a suspension of mind, rather than by the use of mind. Mind, thinking, personal judgment, do not promote habits. A genuine thinker thinks always before he acts, and acts always for a reason, and not by a habit of action. Much habitual action, however, has a good reason, is the product of well-matured conviction. Much in every good life is rational habit; still it must be said that that action is most excellent which is not habitual, but led on by matured thoughtfulness.

Another thing is to be said of habits, that they are *personal*. Every man makes his own habits. The farmer's products are not so much his own as each man's habits. Character is not more personal, than habits. True, others may influence us to habits, and parents and teachers may give much direction to action; but before maturity comes, we may decide and are called upon to decide for ourselves what is right and useful for us; and what we accept of early instruction becomes our personal matter. If others influence us, it is because we make their influence our choice. In any view we may take of it, at last it comes to this, that our habits, like our characters and conduct, are our own.

If so, then we are responsible for them and their influence. They are a part of ourselves, make up a part of our weight in the world. They go for so much of what we are—they count in our make-up —they shadow, or lighten our person, ennoble or defame our character.

If habits are our second nature, they are of immense importance to us either for good or ill. And what is a second nature? It is a nature, or custom, or way of action which we make over our real nature—a covering, or garment which we produce and act in—a nature superinduced over our real nature by a continued course of action in one direction. Do a thing over and over and over again and we come at length to do it without thought. When we come to do it without thought, it becomes habit. We learn a trade; when learned much of our work in it becomes habit. We learn to play a musical instrument, when the instrument is mastered, much of our use of it is habit. We talk and walk very largely from habit. Our manners are largely habitual. We have habits of speech, behavior, thought, action and feeling;

habits of self-indulgence and abasement, all of which are the products of our own activity. So much of our life is a matter of habit, that we come to be known by our habits. Indeed, our habits come to be like our every-day garments—our external selves chiefly seen by the world. A great deal of our outward life is habitual. And this fact indicates the importance of looking well to our habits.

Just here comes a matter of special significance to youth, which is that *the most of our habits are formed when we are young.* That old saying that "it is hard to teach old dogs new tricks," is an exact truth. They have their tricks already learned and are averse to learning new ones. We do not expect old men to undertake new trades. Habit-acquiring is peculiar to early years. A child brought up in a family where three languages were spoken, acquired them all as its mother tongues, so completely that it would carry on a brisk conversation in them all with three different persons and not make a mistake of a word in either. Another child whose German father and English mother each talked his and her own language to it, and the child became equally at home in both languages, at the age most children talk one language well.

A German father, in middle life, came to this country bringing a ten-year-old son. The father was an educated man, but he never learned to speak English with any fluency, while his son acquired it readily, became a literary man, a clergyman, and later on the editor-in-chief of a daily newspaper. Such facts show how quickly habits of speech are adopted by the young, and how slowly by the old. And what is true in relation to speech, is equally true in relation to habits of appetite, passion, manner and thought. Nearly all habits are formed in childhood and youth. Who ever knew of the habit of profanity taken on in maturity? There are many profane men whose tongues cruelly mar our beautiful English, hurt the lovers of pure sentiment, and dishonor themselves by their coarseness, impoliteness and cruelty; but they all acquired the unmanly habit in their boyhood, by listening to the billingsgate of rowdyism which had fastened itself to tongues which ought never to have been degraded by such vulgar speech. The best that can be said for profanity, is that it is an unmeaning vulgarity, as much out of place in civilized society as a boor in a literary coterie, or a clown at a funeral. It is simply shocking to hear profanity in a community which supports schools to teach good English and churches to teach good manners. And all the more shocking is it when it comes from broadcloth and gold watches, as it too often does. And how often are profane men shocked at their own profanity when their tongues habituated to such vulgar speech, blurt out unexpectedly in good company, the epithets of the bar-room and the gaming table. The habits of this coarse speech are a part of the patrimony of evil which the boys inherit from a vulgar and imbruited past. Pity the boys, that men's tongues should load them with such burdens of speech. Have compassion on the boys when men fill their ears with this lingual slime of the pit. Help the boys when such habits are their inheritance from the manhood before them.

There is the case of John B. Gough, born in England in 1817, who came to this country when a boy, to show in a frail, yet powerful life, the power of early habit and the manly way to deal with it. He was a poor boy, who learned the book-binding trade. He spent much of his evening time in taverns and drinking places, and very early acquired the habit of intoxication. By the time he was twenty-one this habit had got the mastery of him, and he so gave himself up to it, that young as he was, he became a sot—a ribald joker and clown in bar-rooms; poor, ragged, filthy. He spent all his earnings in drink and became a miserable wreck of young manhood. This tyrannical habit of the appetite which he had allowed himself to form in his youth, held him in its firm grip, a crushed, bloated, miserable man at twenty-

three.   His waste of his evening hours, had fixed
him in the grasp of this destroying habit, as such
waste has thousands of other young men.

About this time, a good man in Worcester, Mass.,
took pity on him and encouraged him to reform,
to take the pledge, join a temperance society and
become a man.   With a great struggle and the
constant help of his new-found friend, he kept his
pledge and became one of the grand men of his
time—a great reform orator, who, for forty years
held the place of a great platform speaker.   Few
have ever surpassed him in power over a popular
audience.   And yet all this time he felt himself in
the grip of his early habit.   He was afraid to trust
himself in the presence of intoxicating drinks, because he knew the old appetite, like a smothered
volcano, was ready to flame up with the least pro-
vocation.   It was a necessity for him to work all
the time for the reform of others to keep his own
reform secure.   Two, or three times, it is said, he
fell away and drank to intoxication, but he soon
roused himself and went to his good work for
others with renewed zeal.   The fact that the early-
formed habit never gave up utterly, that this
made appetite for strong drink could never be un-
made, but that it staid with him. through life to
torment him, deform his manhood and keep him
reminded of his degradation, is terrible to contem-
plate.

Mr. Gough was a grand man; lived a noble life; fought a heroic battle against intemperance; was loved and honored in America and England for his eminent worth; but what a grief that he had to go round the world publishing his own shame, that he had to carry a rebellious appetite all his life, and have always the thoughts of a wasted and degraded youth. What a memory for a good man to have always to torture him! Grand Gough! Poor Gough! He stands in recent history, in the memories of multitudes yet living, a beacon of warning against the early formation of bad habits. How true it is that "a stitch in time saves nine," and that "an ounce of prevention is better than a pound of cure." Mr. Gough's life-long fight with his self-made weakness for liquor, was nothing peculiar to him. Thousands on thousands have the same experience; only the majority go down at last in the fearful battle, victims to an appetite and the temptations avaricious governments put before it which they do not prove themselves equal to resist. It is not only appetite which the drinker has to resist, but the fellowship of associates and the greed of the seller and the government which sells him his license to traffic in liquor and protects him in it.

Of all modern contrivances for mischief on a great scale, this governmental association in the liquor business under the name of "license,"

stands without a rival. It keeps open and pro-
tected, two or three hundred thousand shops in
this country for the manufacture of the drink
habit in the young and the strengthening the habit
in the middle-aged and old. When the greed of
the kind of men who will sell liquor, is authorized
to do it, so that the dramshop becomes a governmental institution, the prospect looks fair for a
great harvest of such habits as Gough had to contend with. Oh, the power of evil habit, what
a consuming cancer it is, in any form it may
take!

But good habit is equally powerful to bless
men. The habit of wasting keeps men poor, and
often leads on to dishonesty, crime and disgrace;
while the habit of economy treasures every day's
earnings, provides for success and usefulness, and
often lays the foundation of a grand integrity and
a broad and noble character. It is as honest not
to waste as it is economical.

Now it is true that our lives are made up largely
of habits—habits of mind, of feeling, of action.
We educate ourselves into what we are and what
we do, and these educated states of mind and
action are our characters. Our characters, therefore, are simply our combined habits, the strongest
ones being dominant and giving color and tone
to our lives.

It is equally true that our habits for the most

part, are formed while we are young, so that we take early the shape we are to grow in.

It is very noticeable in reading biography, that the coming peculiarities by which a person becomes distinguished, show themselves distinctly in the teens. Most men take their shape before they are twenty-one, that is, their habits of mind and sentiment and action are established. The essential elements of character take form in the youthful period. Of course, the thinking is yet crude, opinions are only outlined, feeling is an impulse, purposes are not well defined, principles know little how to assert themselves, but the consciousness of what one wants to be is distinct. All of us whose years have taught us where we are and what we are, remember that we are the legitimate outgrowths of what we were at maturity. We have not surprised ourselves if we have others.

There is a familiar case in modern English biography which finely illustrates this point. It is that of Hugh Miller the stone-cutter and geologist.

He was born in Scotland in 1802. His father died soon after, leaving him to the care of his mother and two uncles. One of his uncles took much pains to interest him in rocks, minerals, shells, ferns, plants, the sea, the tides, clouds, rain, birds, insects, and natural objects generally. The other took equal pains to interest him in history, antiquities, the social customs of the different peo-

ples ancient and modern, which he must learn
through books. One taught him to observe nature; the other to study books and through them
to learn of men. They each gave a bent to his
mind—a habit of observation and study which he
never outgrew, and which together made him one
of the most marked men of his age. These early
habits gave direction to his life.

At the age of seventeen he was apprenticed to a
stone-mason, to learn the trade of stone-cutting.
For some fifteen years he pursued that vocation
with skill and industry, travelling through many
parts of Scotland to work at his hard and dusty
hammering, till he found it was injuring his
health, and he gave it up.

But while working at his trade he did not give
up his early acquired habits of observation and
study. He made the rocks he was cutting yield
to him their secrets. He compared them with
other rocks to observe their differences. He studied their structure and composition. He made
collections of the many varieties of rocks, and the
minerals, and fossils found in connection with
them, and classified them. Then he sought to
learn their histories, and the parts they played in
the structure of the earth, in the soils, and their relations to vegetation. The fossils led him to study
their history and their relations to living species
of animals. Wherever he went he carried his

hammer and chisel. He visited all stone quarries, mines, cliffs, caves, mountains, and everywhere asked the rocks and soils for their stories. And all this while he worked at his trade. But this was not all. His habit of reading was not laid aside. And reading and observing much led him to writing. His study filled his mind with much that he was glad to write about. The rocks became his friends, and learning from them their histories and qualities he wrote of them with great intelligence and enthusiasm.

His life during these toils and studies was not an easy one. He was often associated with coarse, brutal men; worked, ate and slept with them; passed his evenings often in wretched hovels, and slept on the hardest apologies for beds. Yet, singularly enough, leading such a life, toiling on rocks, gathering specimens of them, studying, seeming to love them, in 1829, when twenty-seven years old, he published a volume of "Poems, Written in the Leisure Hours of a Journeyman Mason." "Leisure hours!" Where did he find them? Doing a journeyman's full work at his heavy trade; gathering cabinets wherever he went; reading history, science, philosophy, fiction, poetry, in his spare moments; he yet found leisure hours enough to write a volume of poems.

After this he contributed to the "Inverness Courier" a series of articles on "The Herring

Fishery," which were afterward published in a volume. About this time he became an accountant in a bank, to promote his health, the stone dust being unfavorable to it. While at this he published "Scenes and Legends of the North of Scotland." Soon after he published his celebrated "Letter to Lord Brougham," which Mr. Gladstone said, "showed a mastery of pure and masculine English that even an Oxford scholar might have envied." In 1840 he went into Edinburgh as editor of "The Witness," a journal of a strong and unique character. In a few years followed one after another, "First Impressions of England and Its People;" "The Old Red Sandstone;" "The Footprints of The Creator;" "My Schools and Schoolmasters;" "Geology of the Base Rocks;" and "Testimony of the Rocks;"—all works of great merit, widely read by the greatest minds of all English-speaking countries.

As a scientific writer, he surpassed all the men of his time in giving a poetic life, a vivid intellectual glow to the commonly dry subjects of science. Some of his scientific books are almost prose poems. And yet he was accurate and faithful in the highest degree.

This sketch of this good and grand man, one of the grandest, take him all in all, that has lived in the century, shows the power and use of good habits early formed. Those two habits of the observation of nature and the study of good books, given him by his uncles, joined their forces to make his greatness and usefulness. One made him a great scientist, the other a man of letters.

All young men cannot be Hugh Millers, but they can be as much benefited by early-formed good habits as was he. The destructive power of bad habits is seen in the wrecks of manhood all about us; while the man-making power of good habits, is equally seen in the good men and their grand successes that are the ornaments and glory of all the ages.

CHAPTER XI.

THE YOUNG MAN AND HIS PLEASURES.

FEW things are more important to understand than the relation of pleasure to true life. Pleasure has its place in every right life. It is not to be ruled out as evil. It is not to be frowned down as sensual and unsanctified. It is a fundamental truth that pleasure has a righteous place in hygiene, in morals, in sociality, and in religion. It enters lawfully into the whole of life and holds a large place in the best human society; and yet it is full of danger. It has wrecked many a life, and will wreck many more, because its true use and place are not understood. Somehow it usually occupies the place where the way forks, and one road is right and the other wrong, one leads to success and the other to failure. Always at this critical juncture, if pleasure is taken for an object in life—something to be lived for—an aim and end, it will allure to deceive and defraud. So taken, it is always a dissipation, wasteful and disappointing. It is beautiful in prospect, but wretched in retrospect. But when it is taken

simply for the spice, ornament, sparkle of the genuine and permanent things which make up a sensible and useful life, it is a thing of beauty and a
perpetual joy. The good of pleasure is all in the
way it is taken. The first thing to settle upon as
a principle is that pleasure is condiment and not
food, is ornament and not substance, is glitter and
not gold, is stage-decoration and not a character in
real life. It holds no high place; is no treasure
to be sought for its value; is not riches, honor,
usefulness, strength, peace, plenty, or anything of
permanent worth. It is not, therefore, to be bought
at any price, to be run for as a prize, to be lived
for as an object worthy of human endeavor. It is
to be remanded to its true place as the flavor,
frankincense, illumination of life. The best that
can be said for it is that it is oil on the machinery,
which prevents friction and rust.

There are the pleasures of the senses delightful
and perpetual, and at the same time innocent and
beneficial, when kept in subjection to their true
uses. Agreeable and life-long are the pleasures of
appetite giving constant rest to the plain, hard
necessities of eating and drinking and the labor of
producing and preparing our food and drink.
Immensely costly are the necessities of our appetites. We work for them through life and must
work for them. If eating were a painful opera-
tion, in addition to the toil of producing our food,

and food was acrid and bitter to the taste, sickening to the stomach, and deranging to the whole system, how grievous would be the necessity of eating. But as it is, it gives a cheerful zest to the whole of life. We eat three times a day with such gratification that we never tire of it, so long as we eat righteously; for it must be understood that no righteousness is more exacting than that of the appetite, and no morality more relentless. The sins of appetite are many and great, leading to much sickness, pain, poverty and physical and moral ruin. All the wretchedness and demoralization of intemperance in all its forms of eating and drinking, originate in the perversion of appetite from its use to its pleasure. More time is wasted, more money is squandered, more lives are wrecked, more hearts are crushed, more deeds of infamy are done, more crime is committed, more social degradation is caused, by giving the appetite to pleasure, than by any other mistake, or sin of humanity. More young men start on this road to ruin than any other, and more find ruin here than in any other direction. The start is so easy and gentle in the use of some pleasant drink with only a slight infusion of an intoxicant, as in cider, wine, beer, that it seems the safest thing in the world to drink it, and thus begin to drink for pleasure. Drinking once for pleasure prepares the way for drinking again and again and so on and on till the worst ruin is reached. By the mistakes and wretchedness of millions who have learned to drink for pleasure, the young men of this age ought to learn that the one safe way is to touch not and taste not any intoxicant. A good lesson on this subject is taught in the life of Horace Greeley, the founder of the New York Tribune, as given in Dr. Lambert's reminiscences of conversations with the great editor. Mr. Greeley was reared in Vermont in the early time before total abstinence was talked of, when almost everybody drank rum and cider, with as little fear as tea and coffee. Dr. Lambert says, "One day, in answer to my question, when and why he became a total abstainer, he very pleasantly narrated that in his earliest boyhood, he had seen enough of the effects of alcoholics, and especially in the form of rum and cider, to make him very decidedly resolve, though he had never heard a word about temperance, never to let a drop of that vile stuff enter his blood, and there never did. There was not a family in that neighborhood, and he believed not in the town, that did not keep, nor a man who did not drink, at least the liquors he had mentioned—with the result, a toper in every family. On his twelfth -birthday his mother, who with half a dozen women in town never drank any kind of alcoholics, addressed to him privately the first temperance lecture that he heard. She pointed

out the evils suffered all around them from the
use of intoxicating drinks, and asked him if any
sensible boy would allow such a habit to fasten
itself upon him. When he told her that he had
noticed and thought of all these things long before, and had fully resolved never to taste liquor,
she caught him in her arms, and hugging him to
her, kissed him repeatedly, bathing his cheeks
with tears; then reaching for the Bible she placed
his right hand on it and swore him never to taste
any intoxicating liquors." There is a picture that
ought to hang in every Sunday-school and every
home in the land—Horace Greeley, with his hand
on the Bible pledging to his mother never to taste
intoxicating liquors.

Yet, terrible as is the abuse of appetite, its legitimate pleasures are satisfying and lasting. The
friendly table is agreeable in its time. Eating together is a sort of social sacrament, and earning
and preparing food a consecrating toil. Every
human home is made all the more a home through
the pleasures of appetite rightfully enjoyed.
There is a benefaction in this pleasure so constant
and universal that it proves a divine purpose in
it. We do not make our natural appetites; they
are given to us. They are universal,—all men
have them as gifts not of their own contriving,
but as planned by the Author of their wonderfully
made bodies. Shall we say that this natural ap-

10

petite is wrong, because of this charm of a peren-
nial pleasure in it? By no means. The legitimate
use of every faculty and power of our being is
pleasurable. And the more intense the pleasure
the more useful and sacred the power.

The charm of appetite is much enhanced by the
added pleasures of the other senses, smell, sight,
hearing, and by the pleasures of conversation and
sociality. And the pleasures of sociality are even
more intense than those of appetite. The joy of
social intercourse is a commanding one, almost
omnipotent over many men. Up out of this soil
of sociality spring all the pleasures of the social
affections, the family and the home.

These considerations begin to open before us
the roots of our pleasures, begin to show us how
all the best of our life is springing full of pleasure,
not our senses only but our affections, family relations, and home ties. It would seem that our
nature is planted full of pleasures, that every faculty, affection, sense, is edged and nerved with an
intense pleasure, and that they all work together,
like the keys of a musical instrument to produce
the pleasure-music of our life.

It would almost seem by this that man was made
for pleasure—that his nature points to pleasure
as its aim and end, as surely as the musical instrument is made for music. If this view even hints
at truth, we must be careful how we inveigh

against pleasure and how we restrain our inclination to pleasure and hedge up the ways to it.

But we must be careful to inquire whether this includes the whole view of human nature before we conclude that man is made wholly for pleasure. From what we have considered, we must see that it is difficult to rule out pleasure, that it enters constitutionally into human life and will not depart at any man's bidding.

If we look further, and we must look further, we shall find that appetite is not given for pleasure, but for the support, health and usefulness of the body and through the body of the whole man. As soon as the body begins to live it begins to die. It is subject at once to wear and tear. Its power is soon exhausted, unless it is replenished with nourishment. Indeed, the body is all the time dependent on the appetite to keep up the supply of its forces. The appetite is the recruiting officer, quartermaster, and supply agent for both body and mind in the campaign of life.

The prime use of appetite, then, is *nourishment*, and the pleasure derived from it is wholly a secondary matter. Properly, we eat and drink to live, not for the pleasure of eating and drinking. Pleasure is added to the first and true and whole use of appetite, simply to secure attention to it, to be a stimulating reminder that the wants of the body must be supplied. If it was painful to eat,

men would avoid it as much as possible; if it was
a matter of indifference, neither pleasurable nor
painful, they would neglect it, and many would
die of starvation.   The pleasure of appetite, then,
is a contrivance to secure the performance of the
duty of eating.   It is a benevolent and delightful
contrivance as well as an intelligent and useful
one.

Perhaps there are few better arguments to prove
that man is the handiwork of an intelligent and
benevolent Creator, than this which is drawn from
the pleasures of the appetites, propensities and
affections of men.   Yet when we have made the
argument, and are satisfied with the conclusion
and have studied the philosophy of pleasure, we
must see, that in all its forms, it exists not for
itself, not as a purpose in living, but as a secondary incentive to human activities.   In other words,
pleasure is the sugar of life to sweeten the solid
and necessary food and drink; the salt of life to
season the viands; the spice and condiment to
serve as an appetizer.

Pleasure, then, is not something to be lived for
—not an object to be sought at the sacrifice of
other and better things—not an end to command
our endeavors—not a purpose to occupy the human
mind and employ its powers.   It at best but oils
the machinery, and makes cheery the every-day
workshops of humanity.   Not in any department

of life, does it assume a first place. It does not
rightly rise into a business; cannot be dignified
as an employment; nor serve as a manly object of
pursuit.   In childhood it may innocently occupy
a large amount of time and thought, but not in
manhood.   In the family, children may indulge
in much play as healthful for their bodies and
minds, but not men and women.   In the social
world pleasure may illuminate and gladden human
intercourse, but not be the animating purpose.
Pleasure may properly come in all round and throw
its gilding light over business, marriage, family,
morality and religion, but these things all exist
independent of it—exist for things better and
grander than pleasure-seekers can possibly con-
ceive.

"What," some one may be ready to ask, "do
not men marry for pleasure?" The answer is,
"Very likely many do; but so many as do are
very likely to want a divorce before a great while."
Marrying for pleasure often turns out to be marrying disappointment. Pleasure is an object too
undignified, too trifling, too unbusiness-like, and
unsentimental, and too void of moral purpose and
force to marry for. Pleasure-seekers at the mar-
riage-altar are those who dishonor and degrade it.
Those who eat for pleasure usually get the dys-
pepsia and can't eat at all without pain; and those
who marry for pleasure soon find its edge so

blunted as no longer to be enjoyable. And why?
Simply because they put a secondary thing for the
first. In homely phrase, they "put the cart before the horse." They marry with too unimpor-
tant an object, and hence degrade marriage and it
refuses to give them its natural and hallowing en-
joyments. Treat marriage as a common thing of
pleasure and it will not have much pleasure to
give. Treat it as a holy thing of reason, love and
conscience—as a sacrament of affectionate life—as
a soul-union of consenting hearts for mutual benefit—for an unselfish doing of good to each other,
and pleasure unalloyed will come to gladden and
hallow and crown it.

Marriage of all human estates and experiences
is most pleasurable when it is entered with right
conditions and purposes. But the pleasure must
come in its legitimate way as the result of an
honorable and high-minded union entered into to
help each other, live truly and in genuine respect
for each other's persons and characters. So entered, pleasure comes to garland the union with
the exquisite flowers and fruits of its growth.

All pleasure, to be legitimate and satisfactory,
must come in similarly legitimate ways, as the
fruit of some honorable purpose, condition, or
character. It cannot be purchased, or lived for, or
successfully sought as a primary object of pursuit. Seek it for itself and it will be shy and dis-

appointing. The pleasures of appetite come only, in their best and most helpful satisfaction, to the temperate who intelligently use the appetite for its legitimate purpose. The gluttonous and drunken get only a delirium of pleasure which is followed with the revenges of disease and pain. All living for the pleasures of appetite is mortgaging one's self to Shylock who will foreclose the moment he can get his pound of flesh. The whole system of tippling in alcoholic beverages, and of pampering appetite with delicious and dainty edibles for gustatory pleasure, is a part of a common mistake of making pleasure a primary object of pursuit, which gets its revenges in the misery it entails. This study of appetital pleasure shows the delusion concerning all pleasure-seeking. The notion that pleasure is to be successfully sought apart from the honorable pursuits of life's great aims—in amusements, games, self-indulgencies, in sensual excitement and the fever of animal gratification, is the bane of many a young life. How often is the golden morning of life spent in the pursuits of pleasure, to the neglect of those preparations which alone can open the way to true success and the only pleasure worth the having. A wasted morning begins an unsuccessful day. A pleasure-seeking youth is a poor apprenticeship to an efficient manhood. Early delusions seldom ripen into later wisdom. Falsity does not lead toward truth,

The point here urged earnestly and with emphasis, is, that true pleasure which is virtuous and helpful, is that which comes in good aims and useful pursuits—comes while one is animated with manly endeavors—comes as the good cheer of a life wide-awake for what is humanly honorable and profitable—comes as the exhilaration of a spirit, which like the sunshine, is trying to make everything grow into beauty, strength and usefulness. The idea that a grown-up person is a child and must be amused to keep him from crying, is certainly not very creditable to one who expects to push his way up to useful manhood. The call for amusements simply to kill time and keep a childish youth from grief, must come from a great inward vacancy, of which one ought to be ashamed who means to be a man. Amusement, recreation, pleasure, for itself alone, belong to the child rather than the man. And yet they are things that swamp many men, especially young men. Many young men outgrow the boy slowly, and some never outgrow him. There are not a few gray-headed, fifty and sixty year old boys among us—men who have not yet begun to think of being anything but boys, or at most, boyish men who want to make play the chief thing of life—want to eat, drink, have sport, laugh and joke and call that living.

Boyhood is very well in its place; indeed it is

an institution we could not very well get along
without. And its jollity and rolicksomeness are
in keeping with its hilarious spirit and its uncon-
sciousness of care and purpose. A boy is a per-
pendicular animal, set upright to see how many
shapes it can assume and how many contortions
it can make, and how much it can enjoy its wrig-
gles and roystering. But when a boy passes into
manhood, where responsibility, care, intelligent
adaptation of power to useful ends, is the order,
what belongs to the boy ought to be left behind.
Play is no longer the order, unless it be occasion-
ally for a transient pastime, having in view muscular and healthful profit. Manhood is for manly
things, in which work, business, manly pursuits
should give pleasure. With the coming of manhood there comes to true men, new orders of pleasure—those of business, intelligence, family, usefulness. In this new order, work is not held as
drudgery, nor duty as irksome, nor the steady
pursuit of any vocation as burdensome. These
are the really good things of life in which are
to be found the genuine pleasures of character-
making, manhood-developing, society-ennobling,
humanity-blessing things.

Pleasure, therefore, in all its forms, is to be
ruled out as a purpose in life, and only comes
properly in as the spice for variety, as relaxation
for rest and change, as flavor to give a keener zest

to our pursuits, as sweetening and relish for the solid and useful. So the true way is to make all our employments pleasurable by the cheeriness we carry into them—to make the whole of life one constant source of pleasure, by the wisdom, worth, and warmth of our constantly exuberant spirits.

CHAPTER XII.

THE YOUNG MAN AND HIS AMBITIONS.

THAT old counsel to the young to "aim high," has the merit of practical wisdom in it. There is as much in aiming as there is in shooting. Indeed aiming is the chiefly important thing. The hitting quality is in the aiming. Whoever shoots without aiming may hit somewhere, yet is liable to hit nowhere. Haphazard shooting is uncertain and dangerous. Nobody can foretell its mischief. It is much so in life. Haphazard living, though common, is seldom successful, save in the very commonest ways. Men who live in a haphazard way trust to luck for good results. And men who purposely trust to luck, are gamblers. They voluntarily take the *chance* of success, or failure. Chance is the gambler's method. It is the fool's opportunity, for there is no wisdom in it; and it is the knave's opportunity, for there is no virtue in it. There is no principle, or smartness, either in luck or chance. There is nothing manly in a bright man's putting his power on a level with the ignoramus as he does when he enters upon a game of chance. Luck, chance, lottery, gambling,

all class in one moral order, which men of good
ambitions do well to play shy of. The only good
luck is in good ambition, good sense, and good endeavor. The lucky fisherman is the man who fishes
skilfully. The lucky mechanic is the one who
does good work and sticks to it. The lucky business man is the one who understands his business
and pushes it. The lucky professional man is the
one who is master of his profession. The lucky
man all round is the one who does everything
well. This is the luck in which true men put
their trust. It seldom fails to bring a rich reward.
What multitudes of young men in all the callings
have trusted their all to the luck of good sense
and good work and have been enriched with the
prizes of noble lives and good fortunes.

One of the ways to have good luck is to have
good aims. It is almost certain that every young
man has something in his mind to live for, something which his ambition covets, which awakens
his best endeavors for attainment. Between the
highest and lowest of these ambitions there is a
wide range, that makes all the difference we see
in men. It is men's ambitions that make or unmake them. If a man has an ambition to be a
'clown, it is difficult to make anything else of him.
If one has an ambition to see the world, he will
travel, if he has to do it on foot and alone. If
one has an ambition to study, it will be almost

sure to shape his life. An ambition for business will show itself in that way. An ambition for mechanics will seek some trade and build a life on it. An ambition for the ministry will find the way into the pulpit. A political ambition will affiliate with politicians and be interested in their affairs. A fourteen-year-old boy had an ambition to be a physician, and because he could not have his way at home he ran away to California, worked on a ranch, and borrowed books of the nearest physician and studied by himself. He became a noted physician. Nearly all marked men had an early ambition for the line of life in which they became noted. An early ambition is usually the finger that points the way the boy should take. If there be no ambition for any particular line of business, there almost always is for the style of man one wants to be.

At the bottom, there are two classes of ambitions that are likely to actuate youthful aspirations; one is to be a *man*, in the best sense of that noble word. Our language has no richer word than man, save those which relate to the Author of his being. Man is not a brute—not an animal, but something vastly more and better. He crowns the sentient creation. Among the qualities that ennoble him is *reason*, which makes him a rational, thinking, self-making, and self-directing being. This embraces his knowing, planning, acquiring, growing qualities. By this he works his way in life, creates business, acquires learning, reduces nature to his use, and becomes himself the ruler in the earth.

Another of his great qualities is *affection*, which links him with his fellow, makes him kind, generous, considerate of the wants and interests of others. Through his affection he uses his reason to found society, organize government, enact and enforce law, establish business, education, and the arts and amenities of civilized life. The neighborly relations, the compact of nations, the intercourse of the world, broad and grand and peaceful as it is, are all the outgrowths of human affection. The great commonwealth of humanity which is coming so rapidly to demonstrate the kinship of men and what they may do for each other, is the great natural product of manly affection.

Still better, if possible, and richer in its works, is *conscience*, the highest department of human mentality. This uses affection and reason to institute and carry forward its great enterprises of justice, humanity, and religion. Conscience gives the sense of what is right, just, good, holy, divine —of what is to be believed in, and hoped and lived for. It embraces the whole realm of morality and religion as its own, which it has produced and keeps alive with its animating impulses to right-

eous living. These three—reason, affection, conscience—united, constitute man. They are in
every man; and their union gives a modification
of each—a blending of all in the personality which
we call man. This is what the nobler ambition of
the young man contemplates when he wants to
be a man. Whoever starts out in life with an
ambition to be such a man starts well. This is
an ambition which ought to ennoble every young
man's soul.

The boy wants to be a man; but with the aver-
age boy the notion of the man is one of strength,
skill, power to master. He has no conception of
the man of mind and character—the responsible,
helping, inspiring man. Such a notion of man
comes later, but early enough to captivate many
a soulful young man. And often is the young
soul supremely quickened by the ambition to be
such a man. Such a quickening often comes before the question of business or the place in society is considered at all. It is one of the best signs
of coming excellence. It indicates a right spirit
—an embryo man such as the world is always in
need of. This is a most worthy ambition, and
well is it for the youth who is actuated by it.

But at the other extreme from this is an ambition to be a rowdy, to adopt the manners and
engage in the frivolities of the childish and
unmanly. " My first ambition was to be a stage-

driver," said one who afterward became a State-
driver—in other words, a governor. Many a boy
has coveted the whip and reins of a coach-and-
four. Many a boy has seen glory in a circus-rider,
and nowadays not a few see it in a bicycle-rider.
Things showy and noisy have a charm for a boy's
early years. That many young men o tgrow the
boy slowly, we see in the numbers who hang
around saloons, theatres, shows, parades, and loaf-
ing places, like moths around lamps, and who
spend time enough in such dissipating resorts to
enrich their minds with a good education or their
pockets with a good outfit for business. Too
many are enamored of the rowdy. They like his
twaddle and ribaldry. He seems to them smart,
cheery, and full of good fellowship. And it too
often happens that young men who are well reared
and well surrounded, get delighted and deluded
by the coarse and vulgar flippancy of rowdyish
men.

A wealthy man had two sons whom he furnished with everything to interest them in his
house, yard, and barn, thinking he would beat
the saloon, the billiard-hall, and public resort, in
the better amusements he would afford them.
Yet he was surprised to find his boys, when well
grown up toward manhood, full of desires to see
and associate with the rowdy element of society.
From others they had heard of what was to be

seen and heard in the blinded resorts of the streets, and they hungered for the flash and piquancy of the ruffian and rowdy society of those places; not because they wanted to be bad, but because their young imaginations had become excited by what they had heard of things there to be enjoyed, and because they had not had awakened in them any high ambitions. They had had an abundance of play, but nothing of work, or useful endeavor. Life was to them a play-time, and the world an orange to be squeezed for its spicy juice. Hence such ambitions as they had were on this low plane.

How extensive and influential such ambitions are, may be inferred from the number of men who herd with the sensuous and frivolous and contribute to the support of the haunts of dissipation and folly. What immense sums of money, what countless years of time, what uncounted worth of talent and character, are wasted on such ignoble ambitions! It is a great question as to whether America, for a hundred years the promise of the world, is not to be swamped by the weight and degradation of such low ambitions. Multitudes of the baser sort of men are coming from Europe, and we are rearing multitudes more to join with them, to make the saloon and the sensual life the dominant powers of the country. We are already in a sharp conflict between these high and low ambitions. Externally, it is the saloon, the gam-

11

bling-house, and the resorts of folly and crime on
the one hand, and the school, the church, and the
home, on the other; but internally it is base and
worthy ambitions which are pitted against each
other to lead on the conflict. And that conflict
is becoming sharper and sharper, as the moral
sense of the best men is quickened and the freedom of the sensual is restricted. Good people are
uneasy and anxious in the interest of the children
and youth, and also in the interest of the deluded
and sensual classes. And the prospect of the
daily floods from Europe and Asia makes them
still more uneasy. It indicates an irrepressible
conflict not less vigorous than that between freedom and slavery.

What should be the attitude of Americans
toward these incoming peoples from the oppressed
nations of the Old World? Most certainly it should
be one of Christian hospitality. And the Christian part of our hospitality should lead us to educate, reform, and Americanize these comers from
afar. We have no need of their bad opinions and
habits, no need of the brute from Europe, Asia, and
Africa, but should reduce it to a man as fast as
possible. We should give no welcome to their
base customs and styles of life, but shape our laws
and intercourse with them to their improvement.
Ours is a better country than those they left, and
they should shape their lives to its better condi-

tions and their minds to its better principles. They are our wards to train up to the higher manhood and womanhood of our country. We have a work to do for them to give them our opinions, principles, styles of life. It is not for us to yield to them and carry our society down to their level, but to uplift them to the better life of American citizenship. Our ambition should be, not only for our own high-minded success in life, but for the improvement of all who come to us from elsewhere. They will come, so long as we keep a better country than elsewhere exists; and so long as they come it is for us to make them over according to our patterns of true life. All the indications are that immigration will swarm in upon us from the lower tiers of foreign society, till this continent shall be covered with an immense and crowded population.

Our health and our hope are in the good ambitions of the rising generations of the original American people. Charge the young people with intelligence and moral purpose to be true to the meaning of American life, which is to make and keep a country actuated by Christian morality and humanity, and all will be well. We want youth inoculated with righteousness, in love with pure and humane principles. We want, now and continually, great harvests of such as helped to lay the foundations of our republic. Perhaps there is no better way to continue to produce them than to continue to study the lives and characters of those most charged with Christian patriotism in the early days which tried men's souls. Among those best suited to the theme in hand, none is better than the life and character of John Adams, the second President of the United States. He is a good example to point a moral for our youth, because he was of humble family, made his way slowly in the world, was largely instrumental in securing and organizing our nationality, rose to its highest place of honor, and maintains it in history.

He was born October 30th, 1735, a little more than forty years before the Declaration of Independence. His father was a small farmer ten miles south of Boston, but a worthy man who had worthy ambitions for his children. He was a religious man, deacon of a church, and brought up his family to strict church-going habits. The boy worked on the farm like other boys of his time till nearly sixteen years old. No neighbor saw anything more in this boy than in the other boys of the neighborhood. He did not see more in himself than in other boys. But his father had worthy ambitions for him and wanted to make him a minister. He told the boy so; but the boy thought he preferred to be a farmer. "Well," said the father, "it is time you were at it in earnest; so henceforth take vigorous hold of the work and learn how to be a first-class farmer." But the suggestion of an education worked in his mind while he worked in the field, till it grew into an ambition. And so he told his father that the education part of his project had grown strong in his mind. His father was glad and started him off to school; and in due time to college. He graduated and became a teacher; then a student at law, studying evenings; and at length a lawyer. In college he stood high as a scholar and an honorable young man, and when he was through had a strong inclination to become a preacher. He was religious, and would like the life of a minister, but he had come to distrust Calvinism, and to doubt its being the true interpretation of Christianity. So he concluded that he would carry all his moral ambitions into the legal profession.

His diary and his letters to his friends during this period of his life are full of manly strength and the noblest ambitions that can actuate a young soul. They indicate the fibre of his mind and the nobility of his spirit. They forecast his future. They are strongly intellectual, moral, patriotic, and religious. They foretell the growth and independence of America. They are reading full of bracing health for the young men of to-day. They are found in his "Life and Works" by his grandson, Charles Francis Adams. When he poured out his soul in letters to his young friends on the great topics which were interesting him so much, he had no thought that they would be read by other than the eyes for which they were written. But the children of his young friends found them, after he had lived his grand life, and now the world has them as a rich legacy of his fruitful and noble mind. In all the literature of religion, there is scarcely anything finer and sweeter than one letter to his young friend Cranch, written a little before he was twenty-one. It is a fervent outpouring of intelligent, even poetic, gratitude for the many blessings of life. The letter begins with a complaint of his hard lot in having to teach school through the day and study law at night. Then he immediately checks his complaint and enumerates in fine and fervent language his blessings in this life and points to the richer ones awaiting him in the life to come, and then adds: " Shall I now presume to complain of my hard fate? God forbid! I am happy and shall remain so while health is indulged to me, after all the other circumstances that fortune can place me in."

As a young lawyer he had a long and hard struggle, but slowly worked his way at last into an extensive business, which was utterly broken up by the occupation of Boston by the British Army just before the Revolution.

Then his country asked for and received his services as counsellor, delegate to the Colonial Congress, minister to foreign countries — twice to France, once to Holland and once to England, and finally, President of the United States.

But that in his life which is most impressive and valuable to study, is the noble ambitions of his youthful years, and the generally wise and practical views of life for individuals and nations.

He was on the committee of the Colonial Congress which drafted the Declaration of Independence, but insisted that Jefferson should make the first draft, because he received the most votes, and as he said to Jefferson, "because you can write better than I can." He nominated Washington for commander-in-chief, as he said, "As the man above all others best fitted for the station, and best able to promote union." His cousin, Samuel Adams, seconded the nomination.

On the 2d of July, 1776, after the vote had been taken that assured the movement for independence, he wrote in his diary: "The greatest question was decided which ever was debated in America, and a greater, perhaps, never was nor will be decided among men."

This day "will be the most memorable epoch in the history of America; to be celebrated by succeeding generations as the great anniversary festival, commemorated as the day of deliverance, by solemn acts of devotion to Almighty God, from one end of the continent to the other, from this time forward for evermore."

Mr. Bancroft, in his history of the United States, says of him at this time: "His intellect and public spirit, all the noblest parts of his nature, were called into the fullest exercise, and strained to the uttermost of their healthful power. Combining more than any other farness of sight and fixedness of belief with courage and power of utterance, he was looked up to as the ablest debater in Congress. . . . When in the life of a statesman were six months of more importance to the race than these six months in the career of John Adams?"

And what made them so important? He had his faults as a man. He was strong and knew it. He was imperious and sometimes had little patience with those who could not see so far as he did. His intellect was autocratic in its grasp of great subjects and occasions, and swept on in imperial power over lesser minds, often to their dislike. He was not a popular man. He knew no indirection, or flattery, or even gentle ways of finding fault with things in which he did not believe. This brusque positiveness made him enemies. But yet in his place and way he was a giant for the American cause and for truth, good government, and humanity. And the source of his beneficent power was the good ambitions of his youth. He prepared himself for the magnificent work of his life, by charging his young mind with noble principles and aspirations. And this is the lesson for every young man to learn of this great character. Only a few can reach his greatness, but his principles of action are for everybody, even the humblest. Good ambitions are the making of men, and good men cannot be made without them. It is of the same importance that every man should be led by good ambitions to his best as that Adams should. Every other man has the same interest in life that he had—has a life to live which is everything to himself and much to the world. The aims which lead it give it color and character. Let the young learn this well and they are already half-made into what they should be.

CHAPTER XIII.

THE YOUNG MAN AND HIS READING.

It would be difficult to enumerate all the things that enter into the make-up of a young man's life, help form his character, and work out his success or failure. Of them all, perhaps none are more potent for good or evil than *reading*.

This is a reading age. Almost every one reads. And those who do not read learn much of those who do. Reading makes far-off knowledge so common, makes difficult knowledge so easy, makes scientific and learned knowledge so practical that the non-reading are much enlightened and influenced by those who read. It is next to impossible to live now outside the realm of letters. Type is king. The empire of letters is a limited monarchy which has a mighty sway in the world. We cannot say that love or money surpasses it, for they use the art of letters to carry out their purposes. Letters have come to serve all uses, and be themselves a mighty power in quickening and developing mind and in aiding the intelligence and enterprise of the world.

Men learn much by observation, but far more

by reading. Men are much educated by the keen sense of observation, but much more by reading. Observation intensifies and sharpens a few powers; reading broadens and awakens all to a wider and grander activity. Observation makes a narrow man, for it limits him to personal sight and knowledge; reading makes a broad man, for it gives him the benefit of the observation and knowledge of all men. Reading multiplies a man by all of whom he reads. A blind man is cut off by his loss of sight from much observation, but reading by raised letters, or others reading for him, often makes him learned, intense, strong, and influential. We have had many great blind men through the magnifying power of reading. Many a cripple and physically disabled man has become broadly intelligent by this enlarging power. A marked example of this is William Hickling Prescott, of Boston, the laborious and discriminating historian who in early life, notwithstanding the affliction of almost perpetual and painful rheumatism, and an injury to his eyes which made him almost blind and often shut him in a dark room for months together, set out to become the historian of far-off peoples, a knowledge of whom was to be obtained from foreign languages and from authors whose conflicting accounts must be reconciled by laborious study and comparison; and yet he succeeded, and his histories of " Ferdinand and Isabella,"

"The Conquest of Mexico," "The Conquest of Peru," and "Philip the Second," are so rich and are written with so much spirit and force as to read like fairy tales, and with so much intelligence and accuracy as to secure their publication in all the European languages now used. In his lifetime he became the associate and equal of nearly all the then living great literary men. His life and work, so rich and remarkable, were the product of his reading, not so much with his own half-blind and often suffering eyes, as by the eyes of those he hired to read for him. Under such forbidding circumstances, he made reading and writing the business of his life. He wrote by the aid of an instrument which he invented, something like a gridiron, which he laid across the paper, so as to write between the wires and in a very coarse hand. The power of reading, moved by a noble purpose, to make grand men, has few better illustrations than this of Mr. Prescott.

An illustration on a larger scale is seen in the Indians who were in possession of the American continent, in comparison with the reading men of Europe who discovered it four hundred years ago. The Indians were men of observation, sharp-sighted, quick-witted, governed for the most part by men of strong minds. Many men of much no-bility of spirit and life were found among them; but they remained stationary in their savage condition from century to century, because they had no written language in which to preserve their thoughts and acts for successive generations. The father's acquirements in knowledge and experience could not be kept for his children. There could be no accumulation of intellectual or moral power, no passing on from generation to generation of the increasing capital of mind, morality, and religion which constitutes one of the grandest features of a reading people's history. The savage man accumulates as little mental and moral capital as he does material, because he has no written language in which to treasure up the soul-accumulations of the ages. The Indian of the American woods was no match for the reading man of Europe with his cultivated fields, his mechanism, art, science, literature, government, and their combining and preserving power. The Indian accumulated nothing; the reading man grew from age to age in all the sources of his power. The one, therefore, in comparison, constantly dwindled; the other constantly augmented in all that made him superior. No wonder, then, that the illiterate red man faded out in the presence of the reading white man. It was not because one was red and the other white, but because one was a reader and the other was not. The result was inevitable.

Reading is a way of growing. A reading man

is not only a growing man, but he passes on the results of his growth to his posterity. A reading community leaves a patrimony of intelligence and moral force in its succeeding community, which gives it great advantage in its outfit for life. How rich the patrimony which the Plymouth Pilgrims and the Boston Puritans left to their successors! Behold it now in what the United States has grown to be, not only in material wealth, but in the accumulated power of mind, morals, and religion. What a mighty force for the world's benefit is treasured in the history of the United States as the result of its reading ancestry! Language, with all its mighty power, is utterly inadequate to express any just notion of what has been done for the world by the reading people who have made this country.

It must always be remembered that reading makes writing. A reading people makes a writing people. Writing is of itself an intellectual exercise, peculiarly wholesome and developing. While it develops power, it preserves it and passes it on to succeeding generations. Our great scientists, inventors, discoverers, have put their attainments into books for multitudes to read. These books have become the sources of our history and made it so immensely rich that it has not only become one of the great sources of the world's mental wealth, but it is accumulating more and more rapidly.

There is no doubt but reading and the writing associated with it are immensely profitable in the way of mental and moral wealth, so that the most reading people becomes the leading, governing, and superior people.

But in considering the young man's reading, it is vitally important that he be helped to see that there is a right choice in reading which is everything to him. Not all reading is equally good, and there is much that is positively harmful. Bad reading, like bad living, is worse than none. Evil gets into books as readily as into conversation or conduct. The bad-minded writer puts poison into what he writes, and to read what he writes is to get the poison. Books and papers which are inoculated with evil, poisoned with falsity and wrong, carry corruption into the minds and hearts of their readers. Books and papers which fire the passions, corrupt the imagination, and weaken the moral sense, are as much to be avoided as places which do the same things. Few things are worse than bad books and papers. And one of the bad things about them is that they never pretend to be bad. They advertise for good things. They begin plausibly and lead on, adroitly concealing their moral poison in characters and conduct that mean no good, in arguments that sustain wrong, in statements that are agreeable to the evil-minded, in exciting and misleading stories, in bright but morally dangerous adventures, or in strange, out-of-the-way experiences. As a rule, stories of passion, wonder, adventure, lawlessness, baseness, and crime—stories of infidelity in love, recklessness in duty, irregularity of life, are Dead Sea poison to the young soul. Stories that a young man would not read with his mother or sister are not fit for him to read alone. What one would be ashamed to read in public he ought to be ashamed to read by himself. As a rule, all slang-reading, shame-reading, crime-reading, is death-reading to the young. In this reading age there are few things more to be dreaded than vile literature. It should be let alone as we let rattlesnakes alone. And much of it is not concealed. Not a little of it gets into the daily papers. Our reporters are often eager for bad news, which should never be told unless in whispers, as we tell secrets. Many of them have no moral discretion, some of them no shame, and not a few of them no moral right to parade their indecency on the great forum of the public press. Like other people, they should not tell all they know. Papers, like fair-minded people, should discriminate in favor of what is decent and wholesome in what they say. Perhaps there is nothing to which the young of our time are exposed which is more pernicious than the slime and filth that is spread broadcast by many of our papers. Young men need the discriminating wisdom of age and moral insight to know how to guard themselves against the literary evils to which they are exposed through the papers and books which never ought to be read. If they will read nothing in private which they would not be willing to read to wise and good people in public, they will be safe. If they will guard their minds against bad reading as they would guard their money against thieves and robbers, they will be safe. And just this vigilance is what they need. The young of our time, and especially the young men, ought to have the sympathy of the wise and good on account of their fearful exposure to the corruption and misleading influence of base literature. But, after all, their chief defence is in themselves. They have judgment; they know what is right. They honor what is pure. They realize that our modern life is pictured in our literature, and they can choose the pure and good and discard the base. And so every young man is thrown upon himself to choose his reading as he chooses his company, and rise or fall by his choice.

This they should remember, that the world is full of good books; that good reading is plenty as water and air, and that it is bread to their minds and the nectar of life to their hearts. It is grand to live in such a time. Every young man can have the great and good of all ages for his com-

12

pany. He can sit down with Socrates and Paul, with Galileo and Herschel, with Gibbon and Macaulay, with Walter Scott and Tennyson, with Irving and Bancroft, with Smiles and Holland, with Holmes and Whittier, with any number of the greatest and best men and women the world has ever had, and read their best thoughts and take the essence of their lives into his. Never before were such opportunities offered to the young as now. The world's best company invites them to its intellectual banquet-halls. Our schools open the mysteries of the alphabet to all. And having learned to read, everything else in literature is open to them. Reading is the key that opens the treasury of all knowledge—opens to the empire of human intelligence. An illustrious example may serve to make this more impressive. One of the greatest readers and most conspicuous men of the generation now passed away was Horace Greeley, the founder and editor of the New York *Tribune*. A little sketch of his life will show how he used the reading-key to open the way to a wide knowledge and a grand life.

He was born in Amherst, N. H., February 3d, 1811, on a small and very poor farm, so rocky and unfertile that it had to be sold by the sheriff to pay the debts of his father when Horace was twelve years old. The family moved to West Haven, Vt., to try another tug to get a living out of a reluctant soil; where, till Horace was sixteen, he worked at farming in the old, hard way. He was a sickly boy, which interfered much with his work. He learned to read very early, and having got the key to knowledge, he read with greedy pleasure all the books within his reach which could give him useful information. Books became his most valued friends. He lived with them, devoured them, found his chief pleasure in them. Of course in such a poor family, in those early times, there were but a few books, and few to be borrowed, and those few were the plain, solid kind. He did not see such inviting and delightful books for the young as are common now, but read such as he could get over and over again, till he could find another to borrow. So enamoring were books to him that he early conceived a desire to be a book-maker. So at the age of sixteen he was apprenticed to the printer's trade. Now he was like a hearty boy in a ripe fruit orchard; he had enough to read. And he devoured with a ravenous appetite all the books that came in his way. He soon became the wonder of the village for his information, the giant of the lyceum, a sort of reservoir of all kinds of knowledge. He wrote short articles for the paper and set up the type for them himself; thus beginning his journalistic work. While thus engaged, his parents moved to Erie County, Pa., and he visited them twice, walking nearly all the way, a distance of about four hundred miles, for lack of money to ride. A four-times-four-hundred-mile walk to visit his parents, was a pretty good proof of the loyalty of his affections. Such men are usually good lovers.

When he was nineteen the *Spectator*, the paper on which he had worked, closed up and he found employment in Jamestown, N. Y., and in that vicinity for a time. A little before he was twenty-one he went to New York City, and soon found employment. There he slowly but surely worked his way up to be the foremost journalist in this country, and not second to any in the world. The last twenty-five years of his life were years of immense influence. No man in America was more widely known, more read and quoted. His great New York *Tribune* was his monument.

The point in the story of his life which relates to the theme of this chapter was his love and use of reading. It was reading that made him. Reading was his school. It educated him, furnished him with knowledge, gave him acquaintance with men and the world, and awakened, enlarged, and empowered him.

The Chicago *Inter-Ocean* has said this of a certain class of young men: "The young men who sport gold-headed canes, smoke fine cigars, and lounge and ogle in front of theatres, are not the future men of business and influence. They are but the coming drones who will live off the world without making it better, and will die and not be missed." Think of Horace Greeley as such a young man. If he had spent his spare time in such a way, or hunting, fishing, or strolling about the village; if he had done nothing wicked, but only wasted his evenings and spare time in gossip and pleasure, as multitudes of young men do, how little would the world have known of him. Had he done so, the world would have had no Horace Greeley to teach the philosophy of life, to be proud of, and to lead it in journalism, statesmanship, and noble living.

As it was, he taught the young men of America how to make the most of themselves, how to make time, talents, and opportunities all tell to the best advantage, how to make poverty subservient to greatness, how to make labor work out success, how to put character to its high and grand uses, and how to crown virtue with the laurels of honor. And especially has he shown how poor, obscure young men, who have nothing but their own brain and muscles to help them, may become useful and influential and make life's hard side serve them gloriously. It is inspiriting to have such men grow up in humble families. They are lights of hope for the poor everywhere. They say to all young men, "Come and do likewise," and all young

men ought to take courage from their example
and follow them as leaders in the true way of success and happiness.

Of course all cannot become as great as was Mr.
Greeley, even if they follow his example. But it
will do them as much good as it did him, according to their abilities, to be readers of good books
and make a practical use of what they acquire
therefrom. Good and useful intelligence gives
force and dignity to every life. Good reading
helps young men in many ways. It gives them
intelligence; it devotes their spare hours to ennobling acquirements; it augments their force of
character; puts them upon a higher plane of
thought and life; saves them from immense waste
of time and energy on trifling things and dissipating company; and enriches them for the life that
now is, as well as for that which is before them.
Judicious, systematic, and persistent reading is
one way to bring all the world to one's help. So,
read much and read good authors, is the counsel of
wisdom to the young man, and keep it up through
life.

CHAPTER XIV.

THE YOUNG MAN AND HIS HOPES.

LONG ago one of the great poets said, "Hope springs eternal in the human breast;" and a greater than he said, "We are saved by hope." The first is an expression of the natural and perpetual office of hope springing up spontaneously in the souls of men, like vegetation over the earth, to give greenness and brightness; the second intimates the moral power of hope in transforming the mind and leading on to better soul-attainments.

All poets, rhymesters, and song-makers have sung of hope as a half-divine inspiration which makes life not only bearable, but throws over it a halo of charming light and fills it with springing joy and brightening anticipation. It is doubtless true that there is no living without hope. He is dead who hopes no more.

There is a sad undertone in human life, heard almost everywhere, sometimes low and musically tender and sometimes rising to a wail of agony, breaking on other hearts like a dirge of death. It is the sinking of hope; and it opens the way to vice sometimes, and sometimes to hard and cruel sin. Now and then it leads to suicide, and still more frequently to a kind of stolidity of sorrow borne with a martyr's sense of duty through despairing years. There is a low hope in many a soul which gives only the twilight to its life. Pity the weak of hope. They are the children of a misfortune as real and sorrowful as ever comes to men. They live in a London fog and scarcely know what bright sunshine is. They are bereft of the cheer and stimulus of genuinely healthful life, and so are half-living, with energies all depressed, purposes half-formed, everything in the machinery of mind working with deficient force.

To some people there is nothing brings so great an astonishment as a suicide. They cannot comprehend it, because they have never been under the depression of a hopeless condition. To the cheerful, hoping soul it is an enigma. Its only explanation is the sinking of hope into a settled despair. It intimates the use, the absolute necessity of hope to intelligent, moral beings.

Hope is usually supposed to belong especially to the youthful period, but, like other original, mental powers, it is permanent, and wanes only to bring disaster. The story goes that an old lady upward of ninety, was asked how old one must be not to feel the promptings of tenderness toward the other sex. Her reply was, " You must ask

somebody older than I." So it is with hope. It
is a faculty of the mind—a part of man having a
perpetual office. Take out hope from the soul,
and what is left is not man. The mind acting
without it is not sound. The man living without
it is not sane. The science of phrenology beyond
all question gives the correct explanation of it,
that it is a distinct power of the mind, having a
special office and use, without which the mind is
incapable of normal action. Though peculiarly
serviceable in youth and beautiful in its springing
life, it is equally a necessity of all seasons. The
man in the vigor of middle life has that vigor
largely as a contribution of hope, and old age is
made serene and cheerful by its comforting elixir.
As people grow in years and cares thicken and
disappointments dishearten, illusions are dispelled
and all stern realities come in their baldness and
roughness, hope is more and more needed to keep
the heart whole and the philosophy of life up to
the accumulating necessities laid upon it.

Life is a ship sailing over an ocean studded with
island ports; and it is taking on freight as it
goes, and needs more and more the whole equip-
ment of good navigation to carry its ever-increas-
ing cargo into the port of its destination. Any
failure of hope is the weakening of the whole ship
and the disheartenment of the whole crew. Hope
is needed, then, more and more, through the whole

journey of life. How true it is, then, that "we
are saved by hope," saved from disheartenment,
from the surrender of courage, from despair and
the disaster that follows it, from the defeat of
powers nerveless because hopeless—saved from
the ruin of a soul destitute of the visions of anticipated good. If children need it, how much more
do men in the midst of life's battle and in the de-
bilitating season of their second childhood. If it
is the glory of the morning, how much more is it
of the noon and evening of life, when clouds are
more likely to gather and storms are almost sure
to come. Surely hope is for the whole of life and
is an important part of the outfit for the voyage.

Important is it, therefore, that youth should
understand that there must be no disheartenment, no sinking of courage, no weakening of
knees, no hesitation in pushing forward for what
is true and right and good, no compromising with
evil because the way to good is for the present
hedged up, no selling out of the best things for
the poor prices of worse things. Armed with the
courage of great hopes, the young are to go forward to realize all anticipated good so far as they
can possibly attain it. Hope gives them the sunshine in which they are to work for it. Hope
makes their day. Whatever else they give up,
they are not to give up hope. Whatever else they
get, they are not to get blue. The good cheer of

perpetual hopefulness is their birthright, and they are to hold to it as to life itself. It has passed into a proverb that "while there is life there is hope."

Hope is their birthright; yes, because it is born to them as a part of their mind, as a companion of their reason and their love, as the eye of the soul that looks onward and upward—the prophet of the soul that announces the coming of the better kingdoms. As a wheel in a watch, it has relation to every faculty of mind and every office in life. As the eye among the senses, it overlooks every-thing. By legitimate right it is born to high office in the republic of human powers, has a part in all discussions and decisions, and is a part of the high court of finality, which directs our life. As well put out an eye, destroy reason, or quench love, as to allow hope to be dismayed and the life darkened by its eclipse. As well repudiate con-science and deny the use of imagination in our every-day life, as to dethrone hope and drift in the dark. It is a working faculty—a contributing force in this marvellous thing which we call mind. True, we cannot take the mind to pieces and ex-amine its parts as we can a watch. We cannot measure it as we can a farm or a mill, nor com-pute its force as we can powder or dynamite, but we know it is equally real, and its separate facul-ties are positive powers, which work as essentially and harmoniously together as any piece of mechanism. This mind is our birthright and each of its powers is our birthright; and we shape life and make it by our use of these powers. We know man's body is a piece of mechanism, and we know that in a large sense his mind is a piece of mechanism, the parts of which work separately and in combination to purposed ends. We know that the swinging of a pendulum by the machinery that moves it is not more by law and does not more exhibit a contrivance to an end than do the actions of the separate and combined powers of the human mind; and we know that hope is one of these powers, acting with as much force, wisdom, and utility as any other.

These faculties of the human mind and their combination, their law and logic, force upon us certain conclusions which we cannot resist only as we lay aside our reason:

First, that there is a contrivance in the construction of the mind.

Second, that the contrivance had a purpose.

Third, that purpose had a moral character—was good.

Then these conclusions force upon us a fourth, that that character, purpose, contrivance, existed before the human mind; and still further, that they existed in a personality who was the contriver and who cherished the purpose. Can there be anything more absolute and irresistible than this logic? We cannot more consistently believe in trees, water, rocks, than in mind, its contrivance, and its contriver. Nor can we more consistently believe in these than in moral character; real goodness in the contriver. Here is builded for us the solid, logical foundation for our religion, which we can reject only by becoming illogical and false to the law and force of mind.

And hope is builded into this foundation as one of the corner-stones. It is in mind; it is in life; it is in philosophy; it is in religion, a real, positive, important power. What it is, how it acts, we cannot know. It is one of the mysteries of mind. Its action is spiritual. If we are staggered before it, we must yet believe it, because it is in us all; it brightens every life, stimulates to endeavor, quickens the pulse of health, opens desirable careers before men, and leads them on and on. It is the vital urgency to labor, the quickening nerve of reform, the joy-giving element of life.

Now this which is so essential and such a commanding force in men is a subject of education. Like the intellect and the conscience, it may be instructed. We may give it eyes, direction, character We can teach it to serve our higher interests, to light our way to the best things, to shine within us a sun of good aims and grand endeavors, and keep our steps moving to the music of what is di-

vine.   We are not to let hope be a blind impulse
leading us in false ways and setting before us the
illusions of the senses and the infatuations of the
passions, but to make it an educated illuminator
of the soul in its best moods, a trained star-gazer
whose look is always upward and whose help is to
lead us in ascending ways.

And it is in just this that hope is of vast interest to the young.   It is a painter and fills young
souls with pictures; and it is for them to order
the pictures and oversee their execution.   If they
order pictures of truth for the intellect, or of
moral excellence for the conscience, or of base
life for the passions, hope will prepare them and
color them to suit the sentiment which makes the
order.   Every young soul makes choice of what it
will hope for.   What is hoped for is the inmost
test of character.   This choice of what shall be
hoped for is the soul's choice of virtue or vice,
right or wrong, good or evil.   In this choice lie all
the moralities of life.   As a rule, men hope out of
their desires, out of their prevailing conditions of
mind, out of what they really are; so, to elevate
and educate hope they must train the mind to
better thought and the heart to better sentiment.
The man must be schooled in fairness, manliness,
rightness all round.   It is a great thing to so train
a man that his hopes are all pure and manly in
the best sense of manliness.

Two conclusions are clear on this subject, which are, first, that we should direct all hope to worthy objects—so shall the animus and aroma of those objects fill the mind; so shall the mind grow like the objects it covets; so shall hope always lead to what is good. The second conclusion is that we should hold fast to hope, stand by it, keep it vig-- orous and commanding, and so keep off the "blues," keep despair at bay, make despondency impossible. "The blues"—how they eat the cour- age out of a man! Blue hours are lost hours. They sap the foundations of manhod; they honey- comb character; they suck the blood out of men's souls. A man with the blues is demoralized, is sick at heart. Next to actual sin, the blues are to be deprecated. All that is good in a man should he rouse up to action to keep up a cheerful cour- age.

Men of great excellence and success are always men of hope. This gives them spring, courage, working force, and holds them steadily to the good things they deem worthy of their pursuit. Hope is a larger element in success and greatness than most men have supposed. Its mighty ser- vice is in keeping body and mind at their best.

The great man whom Americans delight to hold as "the father of his country," who for eminent worth and good fortune has had no superior, was a man of most hopeful disposition. He saw the

end from the beginning, and kept the vision of
the great result constantly before him. Not for
personal ambition, but for the good of mankind
which he foresaw in a government by the people,
did he take up the sword against English rule in
the American colonies. Nothing but the unconquerable hope of securing this good sustained him
through the dark days of the Revolution. When
strong men were despairing all around him; when
multitudes of the people were seemingly indifferent to the great struggle for independence; when
Congress did little but find fault; when his soldiers were unpaid, unclothed, and unfed, his officers in selfish wrangles over their own prefer-
ment, battles going against him, reinforcements of
his enemy coming from abroad, the Tories re-
joicing all about him and doing his cause more
harm than his enemies in the field, and tried
friends giving up one after another and buying
their safety of the enemy, he still kept up hope
and courage, and his fertility of mind and power
to comprehend the great issue and provide for its
necessities seemed to increase with his difficulties.
And so he kept up year after year. When one
of his able generals sold himself and attempted
to sell the cause to the enemy, he said: "Whom
can we trust?" This was the most like a momen-
tary giving way that he was ever known to show.
It seems to be true that the greatest of his great-

ness was his hope, which rose with its trials and helped him, above all his other powers, to be the extraordinary man he was. Through his whole life he was a resolute embodiment of a grand moral and religious hope.

Another example of a hope just about as steady and exalted was his coadjutor and most clear-minded and powerful supporter, John Adams. Seeing always the end from the beginning, comprehending perfectly the principles involved, understanding the resources of both England and the colonies, and knowing the spirit of other nations, he looked forward from his youth to the building up of a great empire of freedom on the American soil, and never for a moment, during the long struggle, seemed to doubt the final result. He had confidence in the principles, the people, and the Providence over all, and so his hope was like a sun shining in his pathway, making it luminous with a coming success.

Another example of a similarly powerful hope was Thomas Jefferson. Very different from both the others, neither a military man nor an orator, but a classical scholar, a lover of books and literary men, a brilliant writer and a strong political thinker, his hope was much like that of his two great compatriots. He was the last of the three men of great hope to rise up and join in the conflict for country and humanity, but, like the others,

13

he was a man of unconquerable hope. His whole life was marked with this quality, so much so that many have regarded him as Utopian and unpractical, yet it held him fast to the American cause and made him one of the great men of the world.

But what was true of these great men in those great times was equally true of multitudes of unknown men who were led by a great moral and religious hope to do equally worthy deeds, and in their places to live equally worthy lives.

Hope is always a leading element in all reforms and reformers, in all advance movements, in discoveries, inventions, improvements. It quickens the desire for and leads on to all best things. It is always dissatisfied with the present and leads on to something better. Mr. Edward Bellamy's book, entitled "Looking Backward," that is just now exciting such wide interest, is an inspiration of hope. It is really a look forward to a greatly improved condition of society. It kindles hope in its readers, and so is enjoyed as a feast of coming good.

Hope is one of the great educators of men. It quickens to scholarship, to all the good attained through education. It founds schools and colleges, makes books, evolves sciences, plants institutions, stirs the masses of the people with business and moral enterprises, and lifts the world out of the ruts of all antiquated things. It is ever on the alert for something new and better than we have had. The most of the new things are the children of hope. In a word, it is the great mental light that gives daytime to humanity's life — is the smile of God. It is an animating element of our religion, which always incites to better and better and looks to the future for the good the present denies, to God for what men cannot give.

Nothing is more important for the young to know early than that they must hope on and hope ever. If they make a mistake, they must rectify it and go on and learn by it not to make another like it. If they fall, they must jump up and in good cheer push on. If they fail, they must not cry about it, but try again. A man of the last generation in Boston failed three times for more than he was worth, and yet paid all and endowed a college, besides enriching his heirs when he died. Hope is one of the never-give-up, never-tire-out qualities. It is never sulky nor sour; has good cheer for everybody; believes in the present, but more in the future; is always for the best that now is, and pushes on for the best that is to be. Therefore everybody should be full of hope and keep so always

CHAPTER XV.

THE YOUNG MAN AND HIS HOME.

In estimating a man, two things are to be taken into the account, which are the man and his location, or the man and his home. It is difficult to say which is the more important. Man a traveller, a wanderer, a vagrant, and a similar man located in a permanent home and tethered to it by all home interests are but little alike. Man a wanderer is aimless, listless, unaroused, uncharged with any great manly purpose, unstirred by the ambitions and energies that move the noble and home-loving of his kind. "The rolling stone gathers no moss;" "the running hound never gets fat;" "the lever without a fulcrum never gets a purchase," are old proverbs that apply to him with special force. He gets no grip on anything, and nothing gets a grip on him. Man has to be located, tethered, made a part of some locality, before his nature begins to bud, blossom, and bear fruit. It seems to be made for a home, made to identify itself with a place, to use its power on its environment, in order to develop its energies and accomplish its best in life. He is like a tree: remove it often and its life wanes; if it continues to live it does not grow. It must be permanent to strike down its roots and gather support from the soil.

The two specially important things to a man are his *character* and his *possessions*. His character is what he is in and of himself—what he has made himself—what he has put into himself of knowledge, force, worth. It may, in strictness, be said to be his inner possession. This he may carry with him wherever he goes. But even this must be located and known to be estimated. Travelling character is an unknown quantity. Wisdom and worth pass for little among strangers. Character must have a home and stay there to be appreciated.

The second part of a man is his possessions— his home and property—the things he makes his mark upon, is associated with—the things by which he surrounds himself.

A man's home is more than the four walls of his house, or ought to be. The locality ought to be marked with him. He ought to grow into his surroundings, into his town and its affairs, into its people and their interests; ought to grow into his place as Emerson did into Concord, Whittier into Amesbury, Adams into Quincy. How many neighborhoods are known by the names of the men who lived there long ago? The outside of a man is his environment—what he looks upon, is interested in, grows to. A real live man is a magnet; he draws things to him; he goes out into things to mould them and put himself into them. In a sense he makes his surroundings his own; lives not only in his house, but in his vicinity. A man must both *be* and *have*, to be a true man in this world of things; he must be himself and have his home. A man really consists of himself and his home. What is a king without a country, or a general without an army, or a farmer without a farm? That is what a man is without a home.

The biographers of George Washington trace back his ancestry through six centuries to a Norman family by the name of De Hertburn. De Hertburn exchánged his estate for the De Wyssington estate, and his family took the name of the estate—that is, the estate rather than the man had the permanent name. The De Hertburns, henceforth to be called the De Wyssingtons, were a vigorous stock of people, and wherever they planted themselves they gathered and held estates and became active forces in their communities. In the course of time the De was dropped from the name, and later on the spelling was changed to Washington. Two of the family after awhile came to this country and settled in Virginia; and true to the family characteristics, they gathered great estates. They were patriarchal men with large estates, families, and homes. Our George Washington was the richest flower and fruit of this ancient family tree which got its name from its home. It was this home-planting, home-staying quality in the Washingtons which contributed much to their power. Being strong magnets they gathered much in knowledge, in things, and in influence. The home not only gave them their name, but greatly increased their importance and weight in the community. And as they were loyal to their homes, their homes rewarded them with accumulating interests. Their home instincts and home-accumulating industries contributed much to the respect in which they were held, as well as to their real worth. They are an example of the power of men's homes over them and of the part that the home plays in the good fortunes of our lives.

There is another peculiarity about the Washingtons, which is that through their whole history they were loyal to their country—were patriotic and public-spirited. Their love of home grew into a love of the country which made the home possible. The home enlarged into the country and patriotism became the instinct of home love. Country is possible only through the power of home to make it.

Mr. Taine, in his "History of English Literature," takes great pains to describe at length and in detail the peculiarities of the Anglo-Saxon peoples of old Scandinavia, who made up the English and American people. In his description of them he calls them "home-stayers." He magnifies their toils for the home, their defence of home, their rough devotion to the home. Through many pages he particularizes their manifestation of the home element. He details their faithfulness to their homes, the sacredness of the marriage bond among them, their loyalty to their wives, and their generally high regard for woman as elements in their home sentiment. From this "home-staying" characteristic he gets the character-making and nation-building qualities of these great people. Out of the heart of this love of home have come these two great nations of home builders who are rapidly spreading themselves over the whole world.

There is no doubt but the home instinct is the most powerful safeguard of a people. The great evils of society do not originate in the home. There are home evils, but they are not great ones nor general ones. Evil has its haunts in public places. The drinking and the gaming evils which lead and foster all others are essentially public evils. The places that teach boys bad lessons and fill their minds and speech with evil are on the street, in the public resorts, away from home and out of sight of home friends and protectors. Be-

tween the street and the home there is always a
moral conflict. Home is the fort for the virtues;
the street is the parade-ground of the vices. The
keepers of home have to guard chiefly against the
debasements of the street.

There is danger that the old Anglo-Saxon love
of home will be weakened in their descendants,
there is so much in our day to draw men away
from their homes. Travel, business, pleasure, the
settlement of new regions and the growth of new
States, the thousand agencies of intercourse, all
take and keep men from their homes. Not a few
have no homes save those on wheels. In this
much-to-be-lamented absence from home there is
dissipation, waste of time and earnings, evil exposure, and a general loosening of moral restraints,
which in the wide fields of a nation is immensely
disastrous.

This subject especially appeals to young men
in the fact that in the conflict between home and
abroad they are liable to get the idea that the
chief good of life is away from home. Most young
men have to fight out this conflict with parents
and home friends on one side, and the attractions
and illusions of the outside world on the other.
They see so much to allure and delight them on
the street and in the stirring public, that home
often gets to be a hum-drum place, simply for eating and sleeping. Indeed, there are many young

men who use home only as a place for the necessary outfit for a whirl in the public arena. The
contrast between what they consider the stupidity
of home and the gayety of public places is so
sharp as to breed in their minds a dislike of
home. This is the open way to a multitude of
mistakes. This dislike of home and longing for
public pleasures is a moth in the mind, a rust in
the heart, a mildew on the moral nature, which
works evil in many ways. If every young man
could catch and hold the spirit of the dear old
song, "Home, Sweet Home," it would be a perpetual blessing in his heart and on his life.

And right here we may get a lesson from its
author, John Howard Payne, who never had a
home after he left his father's home. He was a
man of talent and of many excellences, in some
respects a genius, who had a passion for the stage
which he would not restrain, though his father
sought strenuously to induce him to do it. He
became an actor; then a writer of plays and operas,
for which he got a poor living. In one of his
operas he wrote his immortal song, "Home, Sweet
Home," words and music, it is understood. His
life was one of wandering. He travelled in many
countries, a stage wanderer, always respectable,
but never doing much for himself or anybody
else, except to write "Home, Sweet Home." He
wrote of what he had not save in memory. He

never married; probably never tried to have a
home. Worn out and weary at length, he died in
Tunis, northern Africa, acting at the time as
United States Consul, about the year 1850. Thirty
years afterward, William W. Corcoran, an aged
and philanthropic man of means of the city of
Washington, who was a friend of Mr. Payne in
his early manhood, had his mortal remains re-
moved to Washington and buried in the country
of his birth, in which he failed to make a home.
His dust rests near Mount Vernon, which the
"father of his country" has made forever memorable by a life at the other extreme, in its devotion to home, from that of Mr. Payne.

Had he devoted his excellent talents and honorable character to the true aims of a manly life,
he might, perhaps, have made his life as useful
and as much honored as that of the noble man
who so tenderly gathered back his mortal dust to
its mother country. Poor, beautiful, brilliant
Payne! In his solitary genius, he is a sad warning to all young men to avoid his homeless, wandering, and almost fruitless way of life. Here are
three characters, in their sepulchres, grouped
around the sacred heart of this country—Mount
Vernon—two of them noble, the third piti-
ful, all of whom illustrate the use and power of
home to the man and the country. So important
is the home to the man, that no man has any right

to expect to secure any great good to himself or
be of any great service to the world without a
home.

And the home is not more important to the
man than the country. As we cannot make men
without homes, no more can we make countries
without homes. A country is not composed of a
group of men simply, but of men and their homes
and belongings. And the homes are such signifi-
cant factors that men are to be counted and estimated in them, and those who are without them
are to be counted as nothing. Properly, the man
and the home are weighed together.

It is easy for young men to see that their hope
of usefulness and satisfaction in life rests largely
in the homes they shall make for themselves.
They are to covet homes, live for homes, be a part
of homes, and hold the home sentiments in them
as the manliest part of them.

Of course it is not expected that young men
will have homes of their own with which to start
the life of manhood. Most young men are poor
and start life with empty hands and pockets. But
they need not be empty-hearted or empty-headed.
They can have homes in anticipation, homes in
plan, homes on the brain. They can start at once
the home-making process, which is earning and
saving the means to make a home. They need
not wait for the sight of somebody to occupy it.

with them. Get the home ready and somebody will be ready to help make it cheerful. They can while boys learn how to make home pleasant, how to care for it, how to respect it, how to behave like men in it, how to earn money to support it, and how to keep wrong and evil out of it.

Young men can learn while they are young and poor, as well as ever, that it is not the size of a home or the richness of its furnishing that makes it a real home. Many a blessed, beautiful, happy home has been made in one room. Then homes *grow* as men and trees do. The safe and sure way is to begin small and work and earn and save and live for that small beginning, so as to make it thrifty and improving. Overgrown and overdone homes go hard. Too much in a home makes it a perplexity. An over-expensive home is a trouble come to stay. An over-nice home is a constant fear and worriment. There is wisdom in keeping the home for its real utilities, remembering always that its prime utility is to be the temple of peace and helpfulness. At once young men can get about and keep about making the qualities and things which are essential to genuine homes. The money to make the home and the character to bless it are the two essential things. The money without the character will make a feast without the appetite to eat it, a home without the heart to enjoy it. Whether humble or pretentious, there can be no home that is a home indeed without the heart to make it cheerful, kindly, patient, and helpful. So the first thing to get ready is *the heart to make the home happy.* The beginning of home is in the heart, and a large part of the joy of home is of the heart. The heart is the great home-maker. "Out of the heart are the issues of life," so out of the heart are the elements of home. Make the heart the fountain of home affections, and the home will come and brighten under its sway.

CHAPTER XVI.

THE YOUNG MAN AND HIS RELIGION.

AMONG the many things that should enter into the young man's life to make it complete, considered in these chapters, the most important is left for the last. Beyond all question, whether considered philosophically, morally, spiritually, or practically, the matter of religion is not to be regarded as second to any other.

Whether the young man is aiming at practical success, intellectual attainments, moral excellence, or all combined—which is far better—he cannot, without irreparable loss to himself, neglect the lessons of religion. Religion in its most definite sense, as recognition of and worship of the Divine Being, is narrow; but in its broad and practical sense, as covering all lines of duty and embracing the ethics of all our relations, it is wide and enduring as life itself. It is in this latter sense that it is here considered.

It is common with many to think of religion as relating chiefly to another life beyond the material things with which we are intimately concerned in the present life, but here it is considered as primarily and chiefly relating to the inmost and real things of the human soul in the life that now is, not less than that which is to come.. It relates to the whole of our being here and hereafter, material and spiritual. It rightly takes the oversight of all our affairs, enters into and shapes opinion, conduct, character, affection, even business. It holds the place of the power chief in command, so that its office is to rule, mould, give shape and quality to the whole of life. It is the regulator, the controlling power and informing spirit. Under this view, a life with religion left out is a vessel without a rudder, is a business without a manager, is a school without a teacher, is a community without a government. Not a few young men, misapprehending the real meaning and use of religion, are proposing to do without it and let life take its chances among the breakers of this world, at any rate, till they are about ready to leave it, as though its office was to furnish a safe way out of the world instead of a safe way in and through the world. Instead of needing religion chiefly as an aid out of the world, it is far better for us to understand that we need it chiefly as an aid in the world. Of course its light is needed in the departing hour, but quite as much in all the hours of life. The dying hour is not the supreme hour of life; the supreme is rather the hour of duty, the hour of opportunity, the hour of choice between right and wrong, the hour of self-denial, of fellow-service, the hour of acceptance of truth, the hand of help from above, the faith in divine principles. Every hour in life is important, and not one should be without the aid of religion to guard it from evil, to lead it in the ways of wisdom, and inform and animate it with all righteous principles. If any one hour is the supreme hour, it is the hour that gives religion the helm and makes its principles all-commanding.

If, then, religion is for life, to befriend it in its needs, to guard it in its dangers, to charge it with righteousness, to link it with humanity and ally it with God, the earlier it enters upon its work the better. Good things are not to be put off. We all admit that education is a good thing, indispensable to the best life. Shall it be put off till late in life? No is the universal answer. It is needed all through life, and the sooner the young mind is trained to its ennobling lessons the better. Educate early is the true doctrine. So give the young mind early to the rule of religion that its restraints and helps may aid it in all life's needs. Religionize the mind early is the true doctrine. To neglect it is to starve it, is to abuse it, is to leave it in the ignorance of natural childishness, is to leave it without the great enlightenment which most of all things can benefit it. What-

14

ever else the young man may put off, may neglect, may consider of least importance, this should not be set aside. Considered in all the higher aspects of life, it is of supreme importance. No matter what place in life one is to occupy, whether he is to be rich or poor, in a conspicuous or humble position, educated or not, he has equal need of religion to order well and bless his life. No place is complete without it, no man is a full man without it.

Some suppose that because there are many differing opinions of religion, it is difficult to determine concerning it, and so give it no heed and go on in life without it. There are different opinions about food, but shall we go without food on this account? There are discussions about dress, but shall we neglect our wardrobe on this account? Doctors disagree about medicine, but shall we do nothing for ourselves when sick on this account? There are wide differences of opinion on politics, but shall this keep us from having any politics? Opinions differ about all our great interests, but this does not justify us in neglecting any. Opinion is not religion, any more than it is food, dress, or medicine. Opinion is an intellectual view of a matter. The matter itself exists independent of the opinions. An opinion about electricity is one thing; electricity is quite another thing. An opinion about the human soul is one thing; the soul itself is quite another thing. An opinion about God is what most men hold, but God is another thing. Philosophers have their opinions about love, but love is so apart from them all that men go on loving with little reference to these opinions. Opinion is solely of the intellect; religion is of another faculty of the mind. Shall this religious faculty be put to sleep and kept forever from activity because men have different intellectual opinions about its productions? It is as certain that men have a religious faculty as that they have a faculty for reason. Shall one be used and the other lie fallow ground in the soul?

Men have a faculty for mathematics, but thinkers differ much about many things in mathematics: shall we people of common sense throw mathematics to the dogs because of these diverse opinions? Shall any refuse to use the mathematical faculty in common life because some men differ about questions that relate to it? No more should any refuse to use the religious faculty in common life and in the common education of the soul, because of differences of religious opinion. The undeveloped intellect makes a fool; any undeveloped faculty makes foolishness so far as that faculty is concerned. Torpidity in any faculty disarranges the balance of faculty activity, and therefore the soundness and harmony of the mind. Torpidity in any faculty is weakness in the whole mind and corresponding imperfection in the life. The natural and sound life of the mind is the equal activity of all the faculties. No principle in mental science is better established. Therefore the inefficiency of the religious faculty gives inefficiency to the whole mind and a corresponding inefficiency to the life.

But the religious faculty is not only a faculty in the mind, but a central faculty in a group of faculties, all of which are allied to it in function and product, and which is the crowning group of the whole mind. Around the central religious faculty are the faculties of benevolence, conscientiousness, spirituality, ideality, and hope, all allied with it in the ideal excellencies they produce in the mind and the visions of pure and harmonious life they would open to us all. This religious group of mind qualities is the source of all religions and all religiousness, all the moralities, all the visions of ideal excellence, which have enriched the literatures and the lives of men. The upper side of human life, the best things known to men, the poetry and praise and prayer and love and nobility of all the ages, have been the product of this religious group of mind powers. This has produced the men great in goodness, the soul-giants who in unselfish lives have set the greatest and the best things before men—the teachers in what is pure, high, and helpful—the saints who have lived on the borderland of celestial realities and yet who have loved their kind with a great uplifting affection. And this, too, has produced the common good found everywhere among men, the kith and kinship of soul which everywhere binds men together and gives them visions of something better in the higher reaches of life, which they anticipate in the mysterious yet fruitful hereafter. Out of this group of faculties has flowed a perpetual river of life among men which has made human society desirable and kept always hoisted above it an archway of heavenly light and hopes. Through this group, too, have come the communions with the heavens which have quickened unspeakable hopes and held men's gaze ever upward for more and better.

This group of religious and moral faculties are such an important part of the mind that to neglect them is fearful self-abuse, is crippling manhood in its best parts, is deforming the character where deformity is most hideous to men of sound minds. Just for fair self-treatment, for harmony of character, for roundness, completeness, every young man should order his life by the great precepts of religion which have gained the approval of all the best ages since the Great Teacher of Galilee announced them to the world. And he should begin this ordering early and do it in the deepest conviction of the solemn realities

of the life that now is and of that which is to
come. Our human life beyond all question is divine in origin and oversight, and is amenable to
the government under which it exists, so that the
most urgent responsibility rests upon us to make
the most and best of it. We have no right to
cripple any part of it by neglect or abuse. We
owe it to ourselves, we owe it to our fellow-men,
we owe it to our Maker, to be complete men, reverent to God, helpful to our fellows, just to ourselves. By what right can we live profane lives?
By what right can we set examples of folly, selfishness, and sin before men? By what right can
we grow up to manhood trampling on the best
things, herding with vileness, and affiliating with
profaneness? By what authority do we befoul
our souls with brutality and give our young life
to sin and shame? Who authorizes us to so live
as to please the irreligious? We must please
somebody in our lives: who shall it be, the godless
or the devout?

Surely man is more than an animal. An animal lives for self-gratification, but man must live
for something more and better if he would prove
himself something more and better than an animal. Religion sets before him the better life
which denies self, restrains the animal nature, and
puts its forces to the service of virtue. Religion
opens a great life of well-doing, of genuine manli-

ness, of soul-development in divine things which allies men with the angels, and men and angels with God, and men and angels and God in a kingdom of everlasting light and love.

Nothing is manlier than true religion; nothing is greater, nobler, happier. And no life is complete or anywhere near its best without it; ay, no life is manly without it.

Of course, in all that is here said of religion, that taught and exemplified by Jesus the Christ is had in mind. In comparison with it no other can worthily bear the name, though all religions attest the worthiness of human nature, its consciousness of frailty, its need of help, its craving for something better than it can of itself attain. The order of life which Christ's religion sets before men as possible to them, the law of love which it elucidates as the supreme law, the unselfish morality which it enforces, the divine immanence and superintendence of wisdom and love in law which it proclaims and the triumphing purpose of the divine goodness in all souls in the immortality of its rule which it teaches, are so charged with all that we can think of as heavenly, that we are left to the necessity of holding this as the perfect and ultimate religion. Of its many interpretations, each one must, of course, be his own judge. But considering how different and in many doctrines how opposite are many of these interpretations, it is wonderful how in them all, at heart, is one spirit, one all-prevailing love that wins to righteousness and peace. Or perhaps it may be more proper to say that at the bottom of all interpretations are three prevailing loves, for righteousness, for humanity, and for God, and the combination of these constitutes its spirit. To hold this religion under any of its interpretations is to have a supreme authority, a law of duty and a life of love perpetually over and in one to give dignity, order, and high purpose to living.

Now, to live without this religion is a species of perpetual self-robbery. It is tethering one's self to the earth. This religion gives an ideal of a true life without which no one should attempt to live. It furnishes a wisdom which every one constantly needs. It furnishes the most wholesome restraints, and the most ennobling incentives to uprightness in all our relations.

And what is more, nothing has been found as a substitute for it. No philosophy, no science, no law, no learning, no combination of human inventions, will serve in its stead as a sure director of human energies to their highest uses. It is a light from above, a leaven put into humanity from the Divine, adapted to our nature and needs, and so adapted as to serve us in all our experiences, in joy and sorrow, in health and sickness, at home and abroad, in plenty and want, in prosperity and adversity, in business and pleasure, in temporal and spiritual affairs.

In the fifteen preceding chapters of this book, life has been looked at in a great variety of relations, but not one of them but needs the aid of religion to make it what it should be.

It is a mistake to suppose that religion is only for emergencies, for the stresses and trials of life, for the dark, hard places; it is equally for all places. It is a law, a righteousness, an ordered spirit for the whole of life, and for life in the world beyond the present, not less than for this. It has all life and all worlds for its own. It looks on beyond death into the eternal ages. Indeed, it is above death and is the law of eternal life. It is put in the New Testament as " the eternal life " —the everlasting good of being.

No young man should forget for a moment that religion, as well as all other good things in this world, is soon to become the sole possession of those who are now young. What will they do with it? What for it? How is it to fare in their hands? What are to be its works and triumphs under their direction? Whom will it reach with its blessings under their administration? They are to be its preachers, administrators, supporters, believers, and exemplars. Who is getting ready for the work it will have need to have done in its behalf? Who are seriously weighing their obligations to it? Its literature must be written, its churches and schools conducted, its laws enacted and enforced, its society cared for. Who will do it? Those now engaged in these high affairs will soon be gone. All the great affairs of church, as well as state and home and society, will soon be in hands which are now young. Is there not need of serious counsel with the young about what they are to do and how do it? We who are older cannot be too anxious for the young. Sermons, lectures, books for the young are always in time, for the affairs of life are slipping fast from older to younger hands. Great preparation is needed for great duties, much counsel about important affairs. The young have no choice about whether they will grow old or not. The years come without their bidding. Responsibilities hurry to weight them down. They surely need all the helps of their seniors, all the aids of religion, to make them equal to the duties they cannot shirk. Let them reverently accept the inevitable and religiously prepare to bear the ark of all good through the wilderness of this world to the Canaan visioned in the " hope that entereth into that within the veil."

Works of Rev. Geo. S. Weaver.

Looking Forward for Young Men;

Their Interest and Success. 12mo, extra cloth, 218 pages, $1.00.

The hints and hits for young men contained in this work are in Mr. Weaver's best style, and relate to his Friends, Business, Politics, Money, Time, Ambitions, Reading, Pleasures, Hopes, Home, Habits, and it is his latest work.

Hopes and Helps.

For the young of both Sexes. 12mo, 246 Pages. Clo., $1.00

This book relates to the Formation of Character, Choice of Avocation, Health, Amusement, Music, Conversation, Cultivation of Intellect, Moral Sentiment, Social Affection, Courtship and Marriage. Steady sales attest the public appreciation.

Aims and Aids

For Girls and Young Women, on the various Duties of Life. 12mo, 224 pages. Cloth, $1.00.

The subjects treated are Physical, Intellectual and Moral Developments, Self-Culture, Improvement, Dress, Beauty, Fashion, Employment, Education, the Home Relations, Duties to Young Men, Marriage, Womanhood, Happiness, etc.

Ways of Life.

Showing the Right Way and the Wrong Way. 12mo, 157 pp. Cloth, 75c.

The High Way and the Low Way ; the True Way and the False Way; the Upward Way and the Downward Way ; the Way of Honor, and the Way of Dishonor, are contrasted.

Weaver's Works for the Young.

12mo, 626 pp. Cloth, $2.50.

Embracing the three volumes entitled "Hopes and Helps for the Young of both Sexes," "Aims and Aids for Girls and Young Women," "Ways of Life ; or, the Right Way and the Wrong Way."

The Christian Household.

12mo, 160 pp. Cloth, 75 cents.

Embracing The Christian Home, Husband, Wife, Father, Mother, Child, Brother and Sister.

Sent by mail, postpaid, on receipt of Price,

Address, FOWLER & WELLS CO., Publishers, 775 Broadway, N. Y.

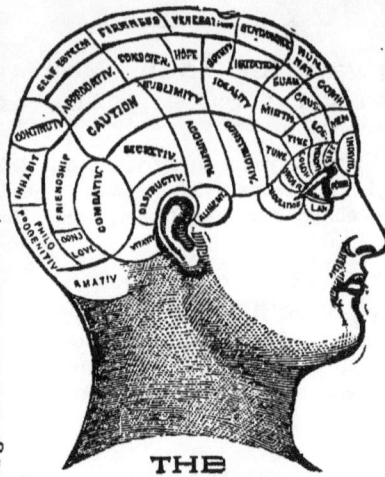

READY FOR BUSINESS;

Or, Choosing an Occupation.

A series of Practical Papers for Young Men and Boys, by Geo. J. Manson, 12mo., extra cloth binding, price 75 cents.

At some time in nearly every boy's life will he want to answer for himself and friends the question : " What work shall I do? What occupation shall I follow in which I can make name, fame and money ?" In this work the author presents what might be called an inside view of the various trades, businesses and professions which are attractive to the youth, considers the opportunities afforded by each, shows what is to be done in order to acquire a knowledge of them, how much education is necessary, and how it can be obtained, the opportunities for employment and the chances for success. It is just what parents need that they may be able to decide intelligently for their sons as to what shall be their life-work, and every young man should read and study it carefully. The following are some of the important subjects considered : The Electrical Engineer, the Architect, Commercial Traveler, Banker and Broker, House Builder, Boat Builder, a Sea Captain, Practical Chemist, Journalist, Druggists, etc., etc., and the learned professions, Medicine, Law and Divinity. The author does not attempt to indicate what is the best line to follow, but rather to show what is to be done and how to do it, to enter upon any one life pursuit, so that when a young man has the matter under consideration he may know what he has to contend with, or to do in order to succeed in that to which he feels he is the best adapted after studying himself and the various pursuits of life carefully.

It will be sent by mail, postpaid, on receipt of price, 75 cents. Address,

FOWLER & WELLS CO., Publishers,

775 Broadway, New York.

PHYSICAL CULTURE.

For Home and School. Scientific and Practical. By D. L. Dowd, Professor of Physical Culture. 322 12mo. pages. 300 Illustrations. Fine Binding. Price $1.50.

CONTENTS.

Physical Culture, Scientific and Practical, for the Home and School. Pure Air and Foul Air.

Questions Constantly Being Asked:

No 1. Does massage treatment strengthen muscular tissue?
No. 2. Are boat-racing and horseback-riding good exercises?
No. 3. Are athletic sports conducive to health?
No. 4. Why do you object to developing with heavy weights?
No. 5. How long a time will it take to reach the limit of development?
No. 6. Is there a limit to muscular development, and is it possible to gain an ab normal development?
No. 7 What is meant by being muscle bound?
No. 8. Why are some small men stronger than others of nearly double their size:
No. 9. Why is a person taller with less weight in the morning than in the evening?
No. 10. How should a person breathe while racing or walking up-stairs or up-hill?
No. 11. Is there any advantage gained by weighting the shoes of sprinters and horses?
No. 12. What kind of food is best for us to eat?
No. 13. What form of bathing is best?
No. 14. How can I best reduce my weight, or how increase it?
No. 15. Can you determine the size of one's lungs by blowing in a spirometer?

Personal Experience of the Author in Physical Training. Physical Culture for the Voice. Practice of Deep Breathing. Facial and Neck Development. A few Hints for the Complexion. The Graceful and Ungraceful Figure, and Improvement of Deformities, such as Bow-Leg, Knock-Knee, Wry-Neck, Round Shoulders, Lateral Curvature of the Spine, etc.

A few Brief Rules. The Normal Man. Specific Exercises for the Development of Every Set of Muscles of the Body, Arms and Legs, also Exercises for Deepening and Broadening the Chest and Strengthening the Lungs.

These 34 Specific Exercises are each illustrated by a full length figure (taken from life) showing the set of muscles in contraction, which can be developed by each of them.] Dumb Bell Exercises.

Ten Appendices showing the relative gain of pupils from 9 year of age to 40.

All who value Health, Strength and Happiness should procure and read this work ; it will be found by far the best work ever written on this important subject. Sent by mail, postpaid, on receipt of price. $1.50.

Address, Fowler & Wells Co., Publishers, 775 Broadway New York.

Men and Women Differ in Character.

[PORTRAITS FROM LIFE IN " HEADS AND FACES."]

No. 1. James Parton.	No. 5. Emperor Paul of Russia.	No. 9. General Napier.
No. 2. A. M. Rice.	No. 6. George Eliot.	No. 10. Otho the Great
No. 3. Wm. M. Evarts.	No. 7. King Frederick the Strong.	No. 11. African.
No. 4. General Wisewell,	No. 8. Prof. George Bush.	

IF YOU WANT SOMETHING

that will interest you more than anything you have ever read and enable you to understand all the differences in people at a glance, by the " SIGNS OF CHARACTER," send for a copy of

HEADS AND FACES; How to Study Them.

A new Manual of Character Reading for the people, by Prof. Nelson Sizer, the Examiner in the phrenological office of Fowler & Wells Co., New York, and H. S. Drayton, M.D., Editor of the PHRENOLOGICAL JOURNAL. The authors know what they are writing about, Prof. Sizer having devoted nearly fifty years almost exclusively to the reading of character and he here lays down the rules employed by him in his professional work. It will show you how to read people as you would a book, and to see if they are inclined to be good, upright, honest, true, kind, charitable, loving, joyous, happy and trustworthy people, such as you would like to know.

A knowledge of Human Nature would save many disappointments in social and business life.

This is the most comprehensive and popular work ever published for the price, 25,000 copies having been sold the first year. Contains 200 large octavo pages and 250 portraits. Send for it and study the people you see and your own character. If you are not satisfied after examining the book, you may return it, in good condition, and money will be returned to you.

We will send it carefully by mail, postpaid, on receipt of price, 40 cents, in paper, or $1 in cloth binding. Agents wanted. Address

FOWLER & WELLS CO., Publishers, 775 Broadway, New York.